# CONTENTS

*An Authentic American History*

# PURITANS'

## A CATHOLIC PERSPECTIVE

# PROGRESS

## VOLUME
## 2

### COMPILED BY THE EDITORS
### OF ANGELUS PRESS
#### MATTHEW ANGER
#### PETER CHOJNOWSKI, PH.D.
#### REV. FR. KENNETH NOVAK

# 1771–1848

# A New Constellation

**ANGELUS PRESS**
2918 TRACY AVENUE, KANSAS CITY, MISSOURI 64109

**ANGELUS PRESS**
2918 TRACY AVENUE
KANSAS CITY, MISSOURI 64109
PHONE (816) 753-3150
FAX (816) 753-3557
ORDER LINE 1-800-966-7337


ISBN   0-935952-35-7  Series
       0-935952-37-3  Volume 2

FIRST PRINTING—November 1996

Printed in the United States of America

# THE FIRST CIVIL WAR 1770-1783

## CAUSES OF THE REVOLUTION

The Christian world in the late 18th century was in the grips of a movement called *The Enlightenment.* Its most radical members believed that the state of affairs in European countries and their overseas colonies, influenced as they were (even in Protestant lands like Great Britain) by the Catholic Middle Ages, must go. God, if He existed, was not interested in men, having created them and then left them alone. As a result, the power of the state churches, and particularly of the Catholic Church, must be broken. Similarly, the authority of Europe's kings must be overthrown, based as they were upon the sanction of the established churches. Such views were spread by writers like *Voltaire* and *Jean Jacques Rousseau.* The motto which summed up these beliefs was "a Church without a Pope and a State without a King."

Adherents of these ideas believed that nations should be ruled by those who had proved their ability to do so–the wealthy. Custom and tradition should be disposed of in favor of "rational" planning; local liberties and differences should be suppressed in favor of centralized rule. In public life, self-interest should replace personal loyalty. Man, after all, was supposed by these people to be merely a rational animal, important only for his money-making ability, rather than a creation of God with a soul.

But these were the Enlightenment ideas in their purest and most radical form—held by only a small minority (although often a rich and influential one). Many other people who would oppose this program if it were made completely clear to them, agreed with portions of it. The large number of pamphlets and books supporting these ideas in more or less diluted form won a large number of converts, and made others at least sympathetic. In time, the whole atmosphere of educated Europe (and America) became more or less influenced by these ideas. This is why the late 18th century is often called *The Age of Reason*, although, as we shall see, application of Enlightenment principles often resulted in bloody and horribly unreasonable acts.

On Christmas Day, 1775, Pope Pius VI wrote a letter to all the Catholic bishops called in Latin *Inscrutabile*. In this letter, the Pope described the ideas we have been talking about. He detailed both their evil nature and evil results. He went on to say that:

> When they have spread this darkness abroad and torn religion out of men's hearts, these accursed philosophers proceed to destroy the bonds of union among men, both those which unite them to their rulers, and those which urge them to their duty. They keep proclaiming that man is born free and subject to no one, that society accordingly is a crowd of foolish men who stupidly yield to priests who deceive them and to Kings who oppress them, so that the harmony of priest and ruler is only a monstrous conspiracy against the innate liberty of man.

Everyone must understand that such ravings and others like them, concealed in many deceitful guises, cause greater ruin to public calm the longer their impious originators are unrestrained. They cause a serious loss of souls redeemed by Christ's blood wherever their teaching spreads, like a cancer; it forces its way into public academies, into the houses of the great, into the palaces of Kings, and even enters the sanctuary, shocking as it is to say so. (cap. 7).

But the Pope's wise warning was ignored. Most of Europe's rulers—Holy Roman Emperor Joseph II, Russia's Catherine the Great, Prussia's Frederick the Great, and Spain's Charles III—believed in much of the Enlightenment (not the part about doing away with the Kings, but in everything that hampered the Church). With the French King Louis XV who died in 1774, most of the Catholic rulers proved their "enlightened" beliefs by forcing Pius VI's predecessor, Clement XIV, to abolish the Jesuits. This loss to the Church of one of her strongest orders was a heavy blow to her and a correspondingly great victory for her enemies.

One especially dangerous means of transmitting these ideas at royal courts and elsewhere was through various lodges of the Freemasons. Although at this time many Catholics and others joined these lodges for social and other reasons, they were unaware of the dedication of the Masonic leadership to spreading the Enlightenment. But in joining they gave the Masonic order the benefit of their time, money, and prestige, and in turn became more inclined toward such ideas themselves. In this way, Masonry became very influential at the court of the French king, even after Louis XV, somewhat friendly to their ideas, died. His grandson and successor, Louis XVI was both much more pious and moral than his predecessor. But he was forced to rely on the ministers and courtiers bequeathed him by

Louis XV, with results that we shall see later.

## Great Britain Under George III

In the British Isles and their colonies, things were more complicated. In any Protestant country, the principles of the Enlightenment were especially welcome. This was truer still in Britain. The reason was that they provided justification for the Whig oligarchy who actually ran the country, whom you will remember from the last book. They already had power; now the Enlightenment made this situation virtuous!

But England still retained the form of government she had always had. On paper, the King functioned much as the American President does. He appointed the cabinet to carry out his programs; just as skill is required for the President to get his bills passed by Congress, so the King's ministers had to be skillful enough to guide legislation through Parliament. In theory, Parliament acted as a check on the King's power, while the King himself provided unified leadership above party and faction. Since Parliament consisted of both Lords and Commons (the latter elected by the well-to-do), both people and nobility were part of the government. King, Lords, and Commons were to maintain a balance which would insure good government as much as anything human can.

However, due to earlier wars and insurrections, as well as the fact that the English throne had been occupied by foreigners since 1714, much had changed. Although the form remained the same, the substance was different. The King continued to go through the motions of appointing the Prime Minister and Cabinet, but in reality the Cabinet was put in place by whichever Whig faction could control a majority in Parliament. The modern equivalent would be the American Cabinet being appointed by the party which holds the majority in Congress. Obviously, if this were the case, the president would have no power over the federal government at all. Such was the case in Great Britain by 1760.

Since the House of Commons members were for the most part in the hire of wealthy oligarchs, and since whichever faction among them was able to give out government positions to its supporters, the whole method of British government changed in reality, even while remaining the same on the surface. Policies and appointments were dictated purely on the basis of keeping a majority in the Commons; corruption grew incredibly, and the national interest was forgotten by politicians intent on wealth and power. George I and George II, being Germans and much more interested in their Electorate of Hanover than in Britain, were content to let things go on in this way. But George III, who succeeded his grandfather George II in 1760, was different.

Unlike the last two kings, George III "gloried in the name of Briton." Unlike them he was faithful to his wife, as pious as an Anglican can be, and more interested in Britain and its Empire than in Hanover. As a boy, his mother had often told him to "be a king." For him, that meant restoring his country's original constitution—in a word, functioning as the president does, rather than as a figurehead. That way, he could lift the government of Britain above petty factional greed and dispute; instead of self-interest, his realm would be governed for the benefit of his people and the glory of God (as far as he could see it). But this project would require a great deal of skill if it were to succeed. After all, arrayed against him were all the Whig factions who between them had complete control of Parliament, however much they might squabble and struggle among themselves when there was no effective King to fear; the owners of the Bank of England, whose control of the country's money supply (an essential part of governing) made them in effect more powerful than either King or Parliament; and those Freemasons and others who were disciples of the Enlightenment.

Against these seemingly all-powerful foes, however, the King had many important advantages. Above all, he was King. In those days, the majority of his subjects had retained from Catholic days the traditional reverence due a King. This was described a century and a half later by John Healy, the Catholic Archbishop of Tuam, Ireland:

> The character of Kings is sacred; their persons are inviolable; they are the anointed of the Lord, if not with sacred oil, at least by virtue of their office. Their power is broad–based upon the Will of God, and not on the shifting sands of the people's will....They will be spoken of with becoming reverence, instead of being in public estimation fitting butts for all foul tongues. It becomes a sacrilege to violate their persons, and every indignity offered to them in word or act, becomes an indignity offered to God Himself. It is this view of Kingly rule that alone can keep alive in a scoffing and licentious age the spirit of ancient loyalty, that spirit begotten of faith, combining in itself obedience, reverence, and love for the majesty of kings which was at once a bond of social union, an incentive to noble daring, and a salt to purify the heart from its grosser tendencies, preserving it from all that is mean, selfish, and contemptible. (P.J. Joyce, *John Healy*, pp.68-69).

The King's coronation at the beginning of his reign, his headship of the Church of England (in Catholic countries the King is instead the defender of and most important layman in the Church), and his continued liturgical role continued to impress upon his people the sacred character of his office, and instill in them a personal loyalty to him very unlike what we Americans feel toward our President. He was father of his country, and most Britons, either in the Mother Country or in her colonies, loved him in a real though distant way. This was a great help in dealing with politicians who inspired in the people no loyalty, and whose only source of power was wealth and corruption.

Secondly, in Parliament there remained a small but compact group of the Whig's long-time adversaries, the Tories. Spiritual descendants of the Cavaliers, their policy was, according to *Dr. Samuel Johnson*, one of their most famous members, adherence "to the ancient constitution of the State and the apostolic hierarchy of the Church of England...." Since this required the closest possible loyalty to the sovereign, the reigns of the last two Kings, themselves creatures of the Whigs, had left them out in the political cold. Many had supported the exiled house of Stuart, at least until their final defeat at Culloden in 1746. But George III's accession breathed new life into them. Here was a reigning King whom they could follow!

However, the Tories alone had not enough members in Parliament to allow the King to form a government above faction. Fortunately, a large number of Whigs were public-minded enough to see the justice of the King's program. They joined with the Tories to form a loose group in Commons called "the King's Friends." For a decade after the accession of George III, this group grew in overall numbers of members of Parliament. Amid factional strife, the King and his friends carefully worked. At last, in 1770, George III and his supporters in Parliament were strong enough to secure a Prime Minister, Frederick, Lord North, who would attempt to run the government along national and patriotic lines.

But the enemy was defeated, not destroyed. The Oligarchy remained powerful in Parliament, in the Army and Navy, in the control of the Bank of England, and lastly in the very intellectual climate of England. They would seek to return to complete power at any moment. If George III were to succeed, it would destroy them; if His Majesty failed, they would ensure that no monarch could ever again challenge them. As long as things went on in a relatively stable manner under Lord North's ministry, they would have no chance to move against the King. What was needed was a crisis. The ongoing attempts of the government to persuade the American colonies to pay a percentage of the money spent on them would provide that crisis.

## The Colonial Oligarchies

None of the colonies were what we call democratic today. With few exceptions the colonial assemblies, upon whom the Royal Governors and other officials depended for pay, and who in general decided the courses of action for the colonies, were elected by those whose property or income qualified them. These constituted a governing class in each colony. Of course they differed considerably from province to province. In New England they tended to be merchants, much concerned with shipping; in religion they held primarily to the Congregationalism their Puritan ancestors had brought over from England. New York's rulers were either wealthy merchants or else proprietors of the great manors. Dutch or English by blood, they held either the Anglican or the Dutch Reformed religions of their progenitors. Pennsylvania, Delaware, and Maryland, being proprietary colonies granted in the first two cases to the Penn Family and in the latter to the Lords Baltimore, their ruling classes were primarily those who had received grants of land from the Proprietors. In Maryland these were mostly English; in Pennsylvania they were a blinding kaleidoscope of nationalities and religions. Lastly, the southern colonies (Virginia, North and South Carolina, Georgia) were uniformly dominated by plantation owners centered in the Tidewater. All in all, they reflected the settlement patterns spoken of in Volume 1.

They were very much like their opposite numbers, the

English Oligarchs, to whom they were related by interests, politics, and often, blood. Developments at home were eagerly followed by them, and they managed quite a civilized life for themselves in the colonies. As with their English equivalents, they were faction ridden, depending on intensely local and personality issues to shape their shifting alliances. From their ranks came the judges, militia captains, and Assembly and Governor's Council members.

Again differing from colony to colony, this ruling class ran into more or less friction with the poorer folk whom it ruled. In the South, where the friction between the backwoods Piedmont region and the coastal Tidewater region reflected the poverty of the former and the wealth of the latter, conflict was especially violent, and broke out in open warfare at various times. The Royal Governors were often sympathetic to the plight of the disenfranchised in a way that many of the oligarchs found extremely uncomfortable.

The attempt of the King and his party in Parliament, and their consequent efforts at re-establishing effective Royal government in the colonies was feared by many of the colonial ruling classes for four reasons: 1) they were political heirs to the Whig tradition of 1688, and believed that effective control of the state ought to be in the best, that is, their hands; 2) many (particularly such as *Benjamin Franklin, Samuel Adams* and *Thomas Jefferson*) were disciples to a greater or lesser degree of the Enlightenment. For such as these, all their activity aimed ultimately at doing away with the monarchy, not just in the colonies but in the Mother Country; 3) there was a great fear that renewed royal authority in the colonies would not merely force them to pay something toward the upkeep of their defense but deprive them of their monopoly of local power; and 4) that such renewal would inevitably force them to share some power with their fellow colonists.

It should be pointed out that at this juncture that the phrase "no taxation without representation" was coined purely as a slogan with which to beat the home government. Most of those who paid local taxes at the behest of the colonial assemblies could not vote for them, and so were unrepresented.

Thus, for those of the colonial oligarchy who were ideologically motivated, the King's attempts were an attack upon progress; for those who were guided by more mundane concerns, they threatened their jealously guarded privilege and power. It was not difficult for them to make common cause with one another, both over colonial boundaries and with their English counterparts. The strong union of many of these Whigs was undergirded by their mutual membership in the Masonic Order, which organization swiftly became as prominent in America as it was at home.

## Anti-Catholicism

Catholicism was hated in all the colonies, and legal in just three. Nevertheless, despite this, and the Penal laws against the Faith in the British Isles, it was continually feared that "Popery" could emerge at any moment to destroy the colonies. In part this was due to the age-long conflict between Britain on the one hand, and France and Spain on the other.

But in New England, the actual spawning ground of the Revolution, it was not merely hatred of the French and Spanish that influenced anti-Catholicism. You will remember that the Puritans had wanted to purify the Church of England of anything remotely Catholic (except, indeed, the Bible). Failing in this, they came to New England. Since the arrival of Sir Edmund Andros in 1686, they had feared that the King merely awaited his chance to make Catholics of them. This was a fear waiting to be exploited.

Worse, when Quebec finally fell in 1760, and was handed over to the Crown by treaty in 1763, George III did not immediately disenfranchise the French-Canadians and hand them over to the New Englanders to run as they chose. Rather, he sat idly by while successive military governors permitted the hated Quebecois to practice their Catholic Faith and live in accordance with their own laws. Instead of putting into effect the Penal Laws immediately, the King was acting as though the newly conquered French were his subjects also! Good Puritans were much offended, as were the Enlightened. This too was a smoldering source of resentment. As Jonathan Boucher said in his appeal on behalf of the King to the Catholics of Maryland, as regarded the New England Puritans:

> Hardly a book or an article of religion has been written, hardly a sermon or any controverted point has been preached, hardly any public debate or private conversations have been held on the subject of religion or politics in which the parties have not contrived a thwack at Popery.

## Hatred of the Indians

If it were bad enough that George III treated his new French subjects so well, his dealings with the Indians were worse. As you will remember, almost all the Indian tribes had allied with the French against the British, save the Iroquois and the Cherokee. But when the treaty with France was signed, George III undertook to occupy the same relationship with his former Indian enemies that the French Crown had had. This meant protecting the interests of his new Indian allies, even against the desires of his white subjects for more land. Hence the Proclamation of 1763, which declared all land West of the Alleghenies to belong to the various Indian tribes; therein no white man could settle without their consent.

Despite this Proclamation, as you will recall, Pontiac and the Northwest Indians rose in revolt. After their suppression two years later, the need to conciliate them even further became more apparent. But it roused a great deal of frontier opinion against the King.

## Summary

The accession to power of Lord North and the seeming triumph of the King's restoration policy alarmed Whigs on both sides of the Atlantic. The bickering over taxes with the colonial ruling classes which had marked the first decade of George III's reign provided a means to ruin his policy. If his measures in the colonies failed, they must fail in England; if he succeeded in restoring the colonies to non-oligarchical government, he would seal the oligarchy's fate in England. In a word, the stakes were not merely the right to tax colonies, but ultimately rulership of the whole British Empire.

Thus was the stage set for a struggle which began in the political sphere, became a civil war, and ended as a worldwide conflagration.

# THE CONTENDING PARTIES

Civil wars are always the bloodiest and cruelest. Brother fights brother, and often no quarter is given. When bound up with revolutionary activity, there is the added ingredient of conspiracy, of the imposition upon the majority of a minority's desire for power. So it proved in that war we call the American Revolution. Every such conflict has three major sides: those who defend the present regime, those who attack it, and those who are neutral. To understand the conflict we are discussing, which has played such an important part in the formation of the American national consciousness, it is well to examine all three sides.

## The Loyalists

These were the defenders of what was at the time the duly established government. To understand them, imagine that a revolt broke out against the government in Washington; which side would you support–particularly if the revolt was led by those who already held most of the power in your state? This was the position the Loyalists were in.

Some favored the King just because he was King; others because they had taken oaths which they would not break. Still others feared being left completely in the hands of the oligarchy, with no King in London to appeal to. Many had disagreed with Royal policy on taxation, but did not see that as cause to commit treason. A few perhaps saw the good effects that would accrue should the King succeed in his attempt to restore the British Empire to its ancient constitution. And of course, there were opportunists, as there are on every side in every question.

The Loyalists were hampered by a great many drawbacks. Firstly, they were not organized on an Empire-wide basis, as the Whigs tended to be. Indeed, they were in the beginning completely unorganized. The movement of events took them by surprise, for seemingly over night the political landscape changed on them. Often, in the beginning, the better educated among them thought that it was only a matter of getting the facts of the situation (that the government wished to impose light taxes in order to offset the tremendous expense the colonies brought Great Britain) out to the public in an effective way. They did not realize that it was not a question of right or wrong, but of power. The majority came from groups and regions effectively left out of political affairs anyway. The one advantage that most supporters of established regimes have–the machinery of government–was of little use to them.

Firstly, there was little in the way of government in the colonies to begin with. Most of what there was–militia companies, courts, assemblies–were in the hands of the oligarchy. The Royal Governors had little in the way of organized support unless there was a garrison of regular British troops in the colony; these were usually too few to be of much use. Loyalists did not begin gathering into armed bands until after the war began; in the meantime, they and their property were at the mercy of the rebels.

It is an exploded myth that the Loyalists were men of wealth. There were some among them, it is true, but most were poor or middle class. They often came from economically disadvantaged areas, or from cultural minority groups. Anglicans in New England, for instance, where they were a minority, tended to be Loyal. But those in the South, where they were members of the Established Church, often were rebels. It will be very instructive to take a quick colony by colony survey of them:

## New Hampshire

Here the Loyal cause was relatively weak. Most lived in Portsmouth, the capital, and were either office-holders or professional men. Typical was the native-born Royal Governor, *John Wentworth.*

## Massachusetts

In New England, due to Puritanism, Loyalist strength was tenuous. But Massachusetts had a goodly number, including the also native-born Governor, *Thomas Hutchinson* and the pamphleteer, *Daniel Leonard.* Although Boston was their hub, as indeed it was of the colony, they could be found in numbers in Portland (Maine, then part of Massachusetts) and Worcester county. Commerce, the professions, and the royal service were their usual occupations, although some few patricians, like Hutchinson, also rallied. Many were driven from their homes to Boston even before hostilities broke out; the residents of what is now called Tory Row in Cambridge were forced to flee one night in 1774, purely for their adherence to the King. The first American black female poet, Boston resident *Phillis Wheatley,* wrote a Loyalist poem:

### TO THE KING'S MOST EXCELLENT MAJESTY

Your subjects hope, dread Sire--
The crown upon your brows may flourish long,
And that your arm may in your God be strong!
O, may your scepter numr'ous nations sway,
And all with love and readiness obey!
But how shall we the *British King* reward?
Rule thou in peace, our father and our lord!
Midst the remembrance of thy favors past,
The meanest peasants most admire the last.
May *George*, beloved by all the nations round,
Live with heav'n's choicest constant blessings crown'd!
Great God, direct and guard him from on high,
And from his head let ev'ry evil fly!
And may each clime with equal gladness see
A monarch's smile can set his subjects free.

## Rhode Island

Here the Loyalists were concentrated in Newport, and were the usual Anglican and merchant, New England Tory sorts. Here again, the Governor, *Joseph Wanton*, was native-born.

## Connecticut

Stamford, New Haven, and Norwalk were the major Loyal strongholds. The Loyalists here were generally modest farmers or professional men. In this colony, even the Governor defected to the rebels–the only one of the thirteen to do so.

## New York

Unhampered by Puritanism, New York was the bastion of the Loyal Cause in the North, particularly among the Scots Catholics and other settlers along the frontier, among the less assimilated Dutch speakers of the Hudson Valley, and people of all descriptions in the New York City and Long Island areas. A few of the great families–the De Lanceys, Philipses, and Crugers, rallied to the cause, as did pamphleteer and clergyman *Samuel Seabury*, the entire faculty of King's College (now Columbia University), and the families of *St. Elizabeth Anne Seton* and her husband.

## New Jersey

Middle-class farmers were the bulk of the Loyalists here, although the Governor, *William Franklin* (son of Benjamin) had a well known name.

## Pennsylvania

This colony too had a great many Loyalists, particularly in Philadelphia and surrounding counties. Here as in New Jersey, they tended to be small farmers if in the country; if German, they tended to be less assimilated. *Joseph Galloway* was the best known Loyalist in the colony. Here were raised two regiments of Catholic Tories, notably the Roman Catholic Volunteers, under Major Alfred Clinton.

## Delaware

Here the Loyalists were scattered throughout the colony, but had a higher proportion of well-to-do in their number.

## Maryland

This colony had a large number of Catholics, of whom most of the poorer sort were Loyal. Most of the population of the Eastern Shore was Tory. In the rest of the colony, Annapolis, Baltimore, and Frederick had the largest number of Loyalists. Prominent among them were *Jonathan Boucher* and *Daniel Dulany.*

## Virginia

Except for the Eastern Shore, (here as in Maryland resolutely Loyal) the Loyalists were most influential in the Piedmont. Few among the Tidewater planters were Tory, although various Merchants and office-holders in Norfolk, Williamsburg, Gosport, Petersburg, and Portsmouth were. As elsewhere in the colonies, the King was popular among blacks, both slave and free.

## North Carolina

Here too, Loyalists among the dominant Tidewater planters were few. But merchants and office-holders in Wilmington and New Bern were often Loyal. The bulk of Tory strength, however was in the Piedmont, among the small farmers called *Regulators* who had revolted against the colony's oligarchy in 1771. Also inland was a large colony of Scots Highlanders settled there after the Jacobite defeat at Culloden. Instrumental in rallying them for King George III was *Flora MacDonald,* who had helped Bonnie Prince Charlie escape Scotland after the defeat.

## South Carolina

In this colony, the same pattern repeated itself, pitting Loyal Charleston merchants and Piedmont farmers (centered in the towns of Camden and Ninety-Six) against most of the Oligarchy.

## Georgia

Most Georgians remained Loyal, perhaps out of grati-tude for the £30,000 annual subsidy granted the colony by the Crown (since Georgia, you will recall was the newest and weakest of the colonies). While Savannah was a Loyalist stronghold, it was also the base of rebel activities in Georgia.

Although significant numbers of the ruling class in the colonies rallied to the King only in Massachusetts, New York, and Georgia, the Tories numbered many talented writers, scientists, artists, academics, and professional men. But at no time did these ever try to cooperate on an America-wide basis, generally fighting and losing their political or military battles locally.

## Catholics Among the Tories

There were only about 30,000 Catholics in the thirteen colonies in 1770. These included the Scots Highlanders in the Mohawk Valley of New York, German and English Catho-lics in Pennsylvania, and English Catholics in Maryland. Four regiments of Catholic Loyalist soldiers would be raised from their number. Many in the Catholic community tended to-ward Loyalism, but the wealthier and more influential Catho-lics (such as Maryland's Carroll clan) sought their loyalties elsewhere. The French of Quebec were also Loyal. Among the better known Catholic Loyalists were Major Clinton, *Fr. John McKenna*, Irish pastor of the Mohawk Valley Scots and later first chaplain in the British Army since the Protestant

Revolt, and Bishop *Olivier Briand* of Quebec.

## The Rebels

The four wealthiest men in the colonies were *John Hancock,* George Washington, *Philip Schuyler,* and *Charles Carroll of Carrollton.* All four were rebels. As we have already noticed, there was a solid core of radicals among the oligarchy who wanted abolition of the monarchy, or failing that, independence from Britain. But in 1770, these were a small minority. Most of the oligarchs would be quite pleased to retain both their connection to the Mother Country and their allegiance to the Crown—so long as these were purely symbolic and did not require anything from them. In this, they were not unlike the Whigs in England. A larger number still did not think in these wide terms, but simply wished redress of what they considered to be grievances, particularly in regard to the Stamp and other taxes. These last were perhaps genuinely loyal to the Crown. Apart from the oligarchs there were various urban mobs, always ready to riot and loot.

The third named group was perhaps the largest, but they were not in control. The tide of events we are about to survey carried them much further than they wished to go, and they were caught between radical agitation and government reprisal. In the end, they threw in their lot with the radicals, who were, after all, well organized and knew precisely what they wanted. It is usually thus with revolutions and civil wars.

It should be remembered again that the Royal government in America was in 1770 considered no more foreign than the Federal government is in California today. Any who plotted to overthrow the American constitution, flag, and so on would be considered traitors. Those who would break their oaths to the Constitution would be considered perjurers. So it was in 1770. This is one other point to keep in mind; each of the rebels who had held public office, like Franklin, Jefferson, *George Washington,* and *Patrick Henry,* had to break their oaths to the King. Such Oaths of Allegiance meant as much or more then as they do to us today.

There was another factor in the decision of many Southern planters to side with the rebels. Most were heavily in debt to British merchants for the sorts of manufactured goods their plantations needed but could not supply for themselves. Hence their support for independence, which would allow them to renege on such debts. This was summed up by Irish poet Thomas Moore:

> Who could their monarch in their purse forget
> And break allegiance but to cancel debt.

As a result of the Stamp Act agitation, the rebels in each colony had two organizations to spread rebellious propaganda and coordinate their activities. The *Sons of Liberty* were a loose organization, somewhat like the Ku Klux Klan or Chinese Red Guards of later years. Their mission was to terrorize Loyalists into submission or at least neutrality, using tarring-and-feathering, burning of property, and on some few occasions, murder, to accomplish this goal. Given that Royal officials could only depend on local militia (often infiltrated by the Sons of Liberty) or the ever too few British troops for security, they were usually unable to protect outspoken Tories, who tended to either keep silent or flee to safer havens. In either case, the Royal cause suffered.

The *Committees of Correspondence* were rather more respectable. These were a network of committees throughout the colonies, often based on the local Masonic Lodge, which served as a conduit of information for the rebels. If a Royal official attempted to perform his duties, word of the "outrage" would soon be spread, in highly exaggerated form, from New Hampshire to Georgia.

Add to these the rebel dominance of colonial government referred to, and it will become obvious that, in a sense, the peaceful continuance of the colonies in the Empire was doomed, if the oligarchs so decided. The assumption of government by Lord North and the momentary triumph of the King's Friends in England promised that the American Whigs would have to show their strength, if their English counterparts were to triumph over George III. War became inevitable, for the King would certainly not back down. But with an administration riddled with Whiggery, how reliable were the tools with which he would have to work?

## Catholics Among the Rebels

If many among Catholics were Loyal, the most prominent Catholics in the colonies followed the lead of the wealthy with whom they were most closely associated. So Maryland's Charles Carroll of Carrollton, and Pennsylvania's *John Barry* (father of the US Navy) and Generals *Stephen Moylan* and *Thomas Fitzsimmons*, all of whom were at least well-to-do before the War, joined the rebels. This would stand the rebel cause in good stead later with France and Spain.

## The Neutrals

Although it is difficult to make any precise estimate of numbers, it is probable that committed Loyalists outnumbered committed rebels. But commitment is an unruly thing–doubtless the lukewarm outnumbered the committed on both sides; such as these awaited the outcome of things before deciding which side they would join. At the end of the war in 1783, however, there were 8,000 American Loyalists in uniform in the British army. Washington at that same time had barely 9,000 under arms, and his desertions were increasing.

Perhaps more numerous than any were those who were

more or less neutral. Some of these were religious pacifists, like the Quakers. Others (and these are numerous in any civil conflict) did not really care who ruled, so long as they were left alone to pursue their own affairs. To use once again a modern example, most adults really do not like paying income taxes. How attached to the government would be those who think of it chiefly in terms of the Internal Revenue Service? How supportive would they be of would-be overthrowers of the government, if they thought that the revolutionaries would charge the same taxes or higher? Either way, they would be most concerned with staying out of such a conflict. Yet it is precisely such people, because of their numbers, who can spell the difference between victory and defeat.

In the case of the American Revolution, it is fair to say that the bulk of the people fell into this category.

## WHAT CAME BEFORE

Due to the agitation against the Townshend taxes on glass, paper, printer's ink, and tea, the Whigs had succeeded in paralyzing the government of Massachusetts and in making the Governor, *Sir Francis Bernard,* return home in disgust. The Lieutenant Governor, Thomas Hutchinson, took his place. Despite Hutchinson's being the fifth generation in the province, he was no more able to restore tranquillity than Bernard had been. Already, the Assembly had arrogated to itself the power to disavow Parliament's tax laws. This would be the equivalent of the State Legislature doing the same thing as regards Congress. But that was only the beginning. As Hutchinson wrote:

> At first, indeed, the supreme authority (of Parliament)
> seemed to be admitted, the cases of taxes only excepted;
> but the exceptions gradually extended from one case to

another, until it included all cases whatsoever. A profession of "subordination" [to Royal authority], however, still remained; it was a word without any precise meaning to it (Hutchinson, *History of the Prov. of Mass.*, p.256).

Local assemblies in Massachusetts replaced the legal administration. In particular, those who persisted in buying the four taxed items (the "non-importation" agreement, you will recall, was a compact by the oligarchy in the colonies compelling merchants not to purchase the taxed items) were ordered boycotted by these assemblies, and subject to assaults by the Sons of Liberty.

## The Boston Massacre

In January 1770, Lord North took office, and almost immediately, events began to heat up.

Inside Boston itself, the presence of *General Thomas Gage* and his two regiments had provided some peace. But on March 5, a mob made up of Sons of Liberty and some others began assaulting a sentry at the customs house. Seven soldiers from the garrison were sent to his aid. Goaded by the crowd (and mistaking some of its taunts for an order to fire), the soldiers fired on their assailants, killing three and wounding eight. This was the famed *Boston Massacre*, which has ever since grown in the telling. The Committees of Correspondence ensured that news of this "atrocity" were known the length and breadth of British America. So infuriated were the agitators in neighboring Massachusetts towns, that they declared they would lead the people in an assault on Boston to drive out the British troops. Since such an affair would have led to great loss of life, Hutchinson and Gage decided to withdraw the troops to Castle William (now Ft. Independence), a fort on an island in Boston Harbor. Shortly afterwards, a local jury absolved the soldiers who had caused the "Massacre" of murder, and found only two guilty of manslaughter.

Ever since the Stamp Act, the radicals had spread rumors that there was a plot on the part of the government to "enslave" America. These rumors were now spread with redoubled force, especially through the Committees of Correspondence and the many newspapers started up for the purpose at this time. Control of the media is key to the success of any revolution. Furthermore, the Massachusetts Assembly spoke of itself in terms up to now reserved to the Parliament in London.

In April 1770, news arrived from London that all of the Townshend taxes had been repealed, except the one on tea. Despite the attempts of the radicals to keep it up, nonimportation died a natural death by July 1771.

Two months earlier, a sort of civil war had broken out in North Carolina. There, resentment at the expensive fees charged for provincial services and extremely high local taxes charged by the Assembly, led the backwoodsmen to rebel against the Tidewater Planters. Demanding that the Assembly's taxation be regulated by the Crown, they came to be know as "Regulators." Although defeated in open battle by the provincial militia on May 16, they remained disaffected. The Regulators would be a primary force in North Carolina Loyalism in the conflict to come.

Apart from the continuing intimidation of Loyalists, and the continuing inability of Royal officials to help them, a period of relative quiet descended upon the colonies.

## The Gaspee Incident

This was broken in 1772. Newport, Rhode Island was a large center of smuggling, engaged in often by some of the leading men of the colony. To rein in this illegal activity, a revenue ship, HMS Gaspee, commanded by Lieutenant Dudingston, plied Rhode Island's waters. On the night of

June 9, it ran aground near Providence. A group of men, containing some of the best known faces in Rhode Island politics, attacked the vessel, wounded its commander, disarmed the crew and burned the ship.

This open assault on the government's authority could not be ignored. A Royal Commission was appointed to inquire into the matter and bring the guilty to justice. But despite the prominence of the affair's organizers, their influence in Rhode Island protected them from indictment.

Meanwhile, in reply to the formation of the Royal Commission, Thomas Jefferson, Patrick Henry, and some others persuaded their colleagues in Virginia's House of Burgesses to appoint a Committee of Correspondence which would be a governmental body. This in turn was to contact the speakers of the other colonial assemblies, and invite them to do the same. All save New Jersey's assembly responded, and formed their own committees. From being clandestine organizations of subversives, the committees had become government agencies.

Back in Boston, the struggle of wills between Hutchinson and the subverted assembly continued, as did harassment of Tories. In the spring of 1773 the connivance of Whigs in England allowed certain confidential letters sent by Hutchinson to the London authorities in 1768 at the height of the nonimportation struggle to be sent back to the Massachusetts assembly. Misinterpreted, they became a great propaganda tool in the hands of the radicals, and were speedily shipped around via the Committees. Benjamin Franklin, then in London as a colonial representative, secured them.

## The Boston Tea Party

May of 1773 saw the passage in Parliament of the Tea Act, which gave the East India Company the ability to sell tea cheaply in America, without any tax upon it. Worse, it would be cheaper than the smuggled tea upon which the income of many an oligarch depended. Thus it was noised about in the usual channels that the real reason for the act was to force the American colonies into accepting yet another chain–this time, a tea monopoly. The Committees of Correspondence ordered the resurrection of nonimportation.

Seven ships filled with tea were sent to America by the East India Company. The two bound for New York and Philadelphia were sent back. The one in Charleston was permitted to unload its cargo, but the tea was simply kept in a warehouse. In Boston, real trouble developed.

Three ships arrived at Boston on or after November 27, and were prevented from unloading by Sam Adams' Sons of Liberty. Governor Hutchinson, despite the fact that not only the Assembly but his Governor's Council were arrayed against him, and although the troops at Castle William were of no use to him, refused to give in to the demand that the ships depart. The radicals, on the other hand, continued to prevent the tea's unloading. At last, as everyone knows, on December 16 a group of the Sons disguised as Indians boarded all three ships, broke open the tea-chests and dumped their contents into the harbor.

The assembly and Governor's Council openly endorsed this action. It was a direct defiance of the Crown. Moreover, it showed that the government had lost all power in Massachusetts, and was fast doing so in the rest of the colonies. For several years, Hutchinson had appealed to King and ministry, informing them of the machinations and plotting in the province, and begging them to take decisive action. Now, at last, they must.

## The "Intolerable" Acts

On March 4, 1774, Lord North asked the King to convene Parliament for the express purpose of dealing with events in America. It must be understood that George and Lord North were confronted with the same dilemma faced by President Lincoln when the South seceded; should the national government act to prevent parts of the country from leaving? King and Prime Minister made the same decision that the President did 86 years later.

Debate over the issue raged strongly. The Whig spokesmen in Parliament, *Charles Fox* and *Edmund Burke*, were predictably against any measures of punishment at all. It was hoped that Lord North would not be able to command a majority in Commons and so be forced to resign. But the seriousness of the situation was obvious to most M.P.s. Between March 18 and May 2 a series of laws were passed, in hopes of dealing with the situation quickly.

The Boston Port Bill closed the port of Boston until compensation was paid to the East India Company for its tea by the people of Boston; the customs house was moved to Salem. Another bill was passed in response to the usurpation of the Massachusetts government by the Adams-Hancock-Otis clique. By its provisions, the Governor's Council was to be appointed, rather than elected. The Governor would now appoint sheriffs and inferior judges, and all other lesser legal officials; town meetings would be restricted, and juries chosen differently. Realizing that any officials who tried to enforce these bills might be arrested by the Assembly, tried and jailed, Lord North put through a third bill providing that any official accused of a capital crime in performance of his duty, might be tried in Britain or in another colony, according to the Governor's choice. The Gaspee incident, after all, had made Lord North suspicious of colonial justice. A fourth bill allowed the Governor to billet troops in buildings other than barracks, should such be more convenient to their tasks. Hutchinson was relieved as Governor, and allowed to emigrate to England; General Gage replaced him.

A last measure was passed, which is particularly interesting from the Catholic point of view. This was the Quebec Act. It expanded the boundaries of the Province of Quebec to include the French-speaking settlements of the old Northwest. Within Quebec, the French civil law was to be retained alongside English criminal law. Rather than an elected assembly, which the French had no experience of, an appointed legislative council was brought into being. Under British law, no one could sit on such a council without renouncing Catholicism—this was the Test Act. The Test Act was made inoperative in Quebec, so that Catholics could sit on the Council. More than that, not only was the Church legal, but it could continue to collect tithes and be given support by the State. In other words, the status quo worked out by the military governors was erected into law, and extended to include all of George III's new French subjects. In the colonies, the King was accused of being a Jesuit, and in a number of towns in America his statues were adorned with rosaries.

In response, delegates from all the Committees of Correspondence except Georgia's convened on September 5, 1774 in Philadelphia. This was the First Continental Congress. The avowed aim was to coordinate resistance to the "intolerable" acts, but the Congress also declared that all laws passed by Parliament with regard to the colonies since 1763 were unconstitutional. The Congress drew up three addresses. The first, written by *John Jay*, was addressed to the People of England, and declared the Congress's astonishment:

> ...that a British Parliament should ever consent to establish in that country [Canada] a religion that has deluged your island in blood, and disbursed impiety, bigotry, persecution, murder and rebellion through every part of the world.

Yet five days later a similar letter was addressed to the

People of Quebec:

> What is offered to you by the late Parliament?...Liberty
> of conscience in your religion? No. God gave it to you;
> ...We are all too well acquainted with the liberality of
> sentiment distinguishing your nation, to imagine, that
> difference of religion will prejudice you against a hearty
> amity with us.

The Congress went on to form an American Association, embracing all the colonies and ordering their inhabitants not to trade with the Mother Country. It declared that
it was in support of the King, so long as he did not do anything Congress disagreed with; and it adjourned on October
26, after resolving to meet the next year, if "justice" had not
been done.

Many objected to the Congress presuming to act in the
name of all Americans. After all, it was in itself formed of
members of Committees of Correspondence, themselves
groups of doubtful legality, serving Assemblies who were
acting irregularly. In Quebec, Bishop Briand examined the
two addresses of the Congress to the English and the Quebecois side by side, and reached the conclusion that continued loyalty to the King who had guaranteed his people their
religion, language, and laws was preferable to alliance with a
group of doubtful legitimacy and intentions.

The Bishop's fear appeared to be confirmed in various
ways. The *Suffolk Resolves*, made by the convention of the
county Boston is in, did not bode well for the Faith, particularly in Article 10:

> That the late act of Parliament for establishing the
> Roman Catholic Religion in that extensive country, now
> called Canada, is dangerous in an extreme degree to the
> Protestant religion and to the civil rights and liberties of
> all Americans; and, therefore, as men and Protestant

Christians, we are indispensably obliged to take all proper measure for our security.

Worse still was the defense of the Congress, *Full Vindication of the Measures of Congress* written by **Alexander Hamilton**:

> The affair of Canada is still worse. The Romish Faith is made the established religion of the land and his Majesty is placed as the head of it. The free exercise of the Protestant faith depended upon the pleasure of the Governor and Council....They may as well establish Popery in New York and the other colonies as they did in Canada. They had no more right to do it there than here. Your lives, your property, your religion, are all at stake.

## PRELUDE TO WAR

While the Congress met, more British troops were being concentrated in Boston, and the town was fortified. Meanwhile, sympathetic groups in the other colonies sent donations and the like to the Bostonians. General Gage, as Governor, dissolved the Assembly on Sept. 28. But the very day that Congress broke up, they met, voted themselves the Provincial Congress, and ordered the militia mobilized and armed.

There could be only one reason to arm the militia: to carry rebellion beyond mere boycott and terrorism into open warfare. General Gage resolved that the stores of ammunition and powder must be destroyed. On February 26, 1775, he sent a small detachment to Salem, where the Provincial Congress was convened; it returned empty handed.

Finally, Gage received news in April that the munitions were being stored in the town of Concord, and with them were rebel leaders John Hancock and Samuel Adams. If leaders and war-materiel could be seized at once, it would break the back of the rebellion. Gage resolved that his troops should march on Concord on the 19th. Given this information, Hancock's and Adams' co-conspirator, *Paul Revere*, after determining that 800 British under Col. Francis Smith would proceed by boat to the mainland rather then by the longer land route, mounted his horse and rode off into the night. He would warn the militia that the British were coming.

# THE WAR

## The Shot Heard Round the World

Although Revere was detained by British troops early in the evening, others spread the word. Adams and Hancock fled to safer quarters, and the munitions were removed. By the time the British advance guard reached the town of Lexington, a group of militia-men or "minutemen" (so called from their having to be ready to fight "at a minute's notice") had drawn up on Lexington Green.

Major Pitcairn, the officer commanding the British advance guard ordered the minutemen to disperse; they began to do so. The British troops began cheering, and a few of their officers fired pistols in the air. This was mistakenly taken to be a signal to start firing at the rebels. The British shot at them, and they ran, leaving eight dead and nine wounded. This was the famous "shot heard round the World," which started the Revolutionary War.

It did not have to. If Col. Smith and his men had marched back to Boston, the countryside would not have been roused against them. Of course, the ammunition would have remained at Concord and the situation which caused Smith's column to be sent out in the first place would have been unchanged. He decided to march on to Concord. Once there, he found both ammunition and Adams and Hancock gone. He waited several hours, and then began the return march. By that time the hundred British guarding Concord's North Bridge were under attack by 300 rebels. Smith came to the rescue, and by noon a pitched battle had developed, with more and more militia pouring in.

General Gage learned of the uprising very quickly. By 8:00am in the morning, Lord Percy with 1000 reinforcements had been sent out, reaching Lexington by 2:00pm. Col. Smith, having disengaged at the Bridge, was now marching back. All along the return route to Lexington, minutemen fired at his troops from behind walls and hedges. Although perhaps no more than 250 militiamen fought at any one time, they had accounted for 273 British casualties. Finally, Smith and his men arrived at Lexington, where Lord Percy and his men awaited them.

In the meantime, the militia had gathered again, and it took artillery fire to clear the road back to Boston. Fearing (rightly, as it turned out) that a fresh militia company would be awaiting them in Cambridge, Lord Percy brought his men back by way of Charlestown. They were only free from sniper fire when they crossed over to Boston. Overnight, the Province's capital became a besieged city, and Royal authority vanished in the rest of Massachusetts.

## The Collapse of Royal Authority

News took a long time to travel in those days, we would think now. There were neither telegraph, television, nor telephone. Couriers by land and ships by sea were the means used to convey letters, papers, and proclamations. It could take up to three months for information to cross the Atlantic. But the Committees of Correspondence were able to get news out through their network as quickly as humanly possible in those days. Thus information about the events at

Lexington and Concord (suitably slanted) was quickly made available, and resulted in the collapse of Royal authority in most of the colonies.

In New Hampshire, Royal governor *Sir John Wentworth* fled from a mob in Portsmouth to a fort in the harbor, and then to England. Rhode Island's *Joseph Wanton* resigned and retired to his home in Newport. In Connecticut, governor *Jonathan Trumbull* not only declared for the rebels (and kept his job) he became the model of "Uncle Sam." All three provinces sent troops to join the Massachusetts militia encamped at Cambridge.

In the rest of the colonies, either subverted assemblies or self-proclaimed Provincial Congresses took control. In some places the governors tried to co-exist with the new rulers. In others they fled. Only Virginia's **Lord Dunmore** attempted some resistance against the rebels, particularly after Patrick Henry gave his *"Liberty or Death"* speech to the Virginia House of Burgesses after word of Lexington and Concord arrived. But he was forced to flee the Governor's Palace at Williamsburg for the Loyalist Port of Norfolk.

Meanwhile, on the night of May 10, **Ethan Allen** and his Vermont **Green Mountain Boys** took Ft. Ticonderoga on Lake Champlain, in the name of "the Continental Congress and the Great Jehovah." Shortly afterwards they took Crown Point. These seizures accomplished two important goals: they opened the road to Canada, and they provided the rebel forces with 183 cannon, 19 mortars, 3 howitzers, 51 swivels, and 52 tons of cannon balls. This was the only artillery available to the rebels, essential if they were to take Boston from the British.

North of that city was the Charlestown peninsula, which contained the city of that name and two hills, Bunker and Breed's. On June 17, General Gage was informed that during the previous night the rebels had fortified the two hills.

The Charlestown peninsula was essential to the security of Boston. He ordered the position on Breed's Hill to be taken. Twice the British marched up the hill, and twice they were forced to withdraw because of heavy casualties. At last, with the rebels having both sustained heavy losses and run out of gunpowder, they withdrew in the face of the third assault. Exhausted, the British allowed the rebels to escape. But the Battle of Bunker Hill, as it is always miscalled, was the first major pitched battle between the revolutionaries and the Royal forces. Among the British dead was Major Pitcairn of Lexington; among their opponents, *Dr. Joseph Warren*, Master of the Masonic Grand Lodge of Massachusetts, who had done so much to bring Massachusetts into rebellion.

A few days before this (although news had not yet reached New England) the Continental Congress had accepted the forces gathered at Cambridge as its army. It appointed George Washington of Virginia, the most distinguished American officer in the war against the French, as commander in chief, as well as five Major-Generals, and eight Brigadier Generals. These arrived at Cambridge on July 2. There to greet them was a new flag. Under the British, the most commonly used flag was the Red Ensign (also called Queen Anne's flag), which bore the Union Jack in the upper corner with a red field. Since at this stage the rebels claimed still to be loyal to George III, and only at war with his ministers (they called the British troops "ministerial" soldiers), they differentiated their flag with six horizontal white stripes. This formed seven red ones in between, which taken together were to represent the 13 associated colonies. The Union Jack was kept in the corner to show continued loyalty to the Crown, and the whole called the "Grand Union" flag. Under it, Washington began the organization from the various militias gathered at Cambridge, of what we must now call the Continental Army.

## The Invasion of Canada

After Bunker Hill, events settled for a while into a sort of stalemate. Apart from drawing up lists of Loyalists to be guarded against in every community, the new authorities were content to spend their time trying to continue with the tasks of administration. The British army besieged in Boston, and still in charge of small posts on the frontier and detachments in ports like New York, was content for the moment to await developments. The Royal Navy's control of the sea gave the British and Loyalist Americans every confidence that they could win by waiting for the rebels to "come to their senses."

Congress had other plans. To break the deadlock, an invasion of Canada was resolved upon. Word had reached Cambridge that Governor Carleton had only 1000 men to hold the whole province. Given that the French were sure to join them, the Continental leadership thought it would be an easy invasion.

It was decided that two columns would set out. A left wing, under *General Richard Montgomery*, would set out from Crown Point and advance north to take Montreal; from there they would proceed to Quebec City. The right column, under *Benedict Arnold* would proceed north along the Kennebec river in Maine, proceeding more or less directly to Quebec City. Meeting Montgomery's army there, the two forces would jointly take the walled city.

What appeared so easy in theory was not in reality. Setting out on Sept. 20 1775 from Ft. Pownal, Maine, Arnold's column marched alongside the Kennebec and Chaudiere rivers. In those days, that area was deepest wilderness. Cold and hunger were so demanding that one detachment of 350 men, led by a Col. Enos, simply returned home. Of the remainder, 75 more died before the column reached the shores of the St. Lawrence on November 8–only 675 men made it out of the original 1100.

But Quebec was reinforced by 200 troops a day before Arnold reached it. Secure within its walls, well provisioned, the city could not be taken by Arnold's tired, hungry soldiers alone–even though they wasted a good deal of powder and shot trying to. At last, having heard that Montreal had fallen to Montgomery, they sat down to wait for his troops.

These had made their way down Lake Champlain by boat. When they landed they were ambushed by a force of French Canadians and Indians, who after some heavy firing pulled away into the woods. The Continentals then marched north to Ft. St. John, where the British and French Canadians were dug in. Montgomery's men dug in themselves in early October, and the two armies fired artillery at each other with little result. But the deadlock was broken when a small party of Continentals captured Ft. Chambly further down the river, thus cutting Ft. St. John off from Montreal. A British relief column was repulsed; Ft. St. John surrendered on November 3rd. Nothing now lay between the invaders and Montreal.

On November 12, Montgomery and his men entered Montreal, Carleton having withdrawn the night before. The British commander then went downriver to Quebec. Between regular British soldiers, French militia, Scots militia, Marines and sailors, Carleton had about 1168 men to defend a city better suited to 3000.

But Arnold and Montgomery together had less than 1000 men themselves. The French Canadians refused to help them, and battle was finally underway by December 31. However, Montgomery was killed, and Quebec City's defenders fought hard. The Continentals lost 48 killed, 34 wounded, and 372 were made prisoners; this was more than half of Arnold's command. He had to think of a way to extract his men from Canada.

## The Fall of Boston

Although Quebec had been saved, and Boston remained in British hands, the King and his ministers realized that if the colonies were to be kept they would have to be fought for. For this, troops were needed. Where to find them? Ireland was a traditional recruiting ground for the army; and the leadership of the Irish Catholics rallied to the King's cause. They presented an Address to the King:

> ...justly abhorring the unnatural rebellion which had lately broken out among some of his American subjects against his most sacred person and government. We hardly presume to lay at his feet two millions of loyal, faithful, and affectionate hearts and hands.

The leaders of the Catholic Committee (which, much encouraged by the Quebec Act was working for an end to the Penal Laws), offered to raise funds for recruiting volunteers in Ireland. The Catholic Lord Kenmare offered to raise 1100 men himself. But not only did the Northern Irish Protestants prevail upon the Cabinet to reject these offers, they would not join the army themselves. Many of their kindred were settled in America, and generally supported the rebels (these were the "Scotch-Irish").

This left the Highlands of Scotland as a source of troops. But there were only so many available. Where to turn?

At first, the government hesitated to arm and supply the Indian allies. But with such a lack of men, it was decided to do so. While this did provide more fighting men immediately, it helped weaken the Royal cause among the frontiersmen, who soon learned to identify the Crown with an Indian terror the British were powerless to control, the tribes being allies rather than subjects.

One traditional means of raising troops the British government had used in other conflicts (including the Jacobite wars) was the hiring of mercenaries. 30,000 troops from small German states (called Hessians from Hesse-Kassel, where the largest number came from) were hired and brought over to the colonies. This too was probably a mistake; while they were effective soldiers, the rebel propaganda machine made much of this use of foreigners to fight British Americans. It made Americans more accepting of alliance with foreign nations against the King.

The best source of troops the British did not consider until it was already very late to organize them: the Loyalists. In every colony these had organized "Associations" of "friends of government." These in turn applied to the Cabinet to be organized as regiments and armed groups to prevent rebel takeover of colonial governments. But Lord North's cabinet was too overwhelmed by the course of events to act on these proposals. It was not until late 1775 that plans of this sort were even considered in London, and it was early 1776 before anything was done. In the meantime, as we have seen, the Royal administrations collapsed.

But Boston remained. If the rebels were to triumph it had to be taken; this was shown by the raid on Portland, Maine on October 17, 1775. The burning of the town served to turn more Americans against the Crown, and gave rise to the false rumor that the British intended to burn all the coastal ports.

Meanwhile, General Gage was replaced by *Sir William Howe.* His hopes were raised by events in Canada, where the Continental governor at Montreal, General Wooster, had outlawed Catholicism. This led to resistance on the part of the French, and the collapse of the American army. What remained of it was led back up to Crown Point by Arnold.

Further, without opposing artillery, Boston could not be taken by assault.

Unfortunately for Howe, the artillery taken at Ticonderoga was on its way over the mountains by sled to Cambridge. Once there on February 26, 1776, it was used to shell British outlying positions. Under cover of this barrage, artillery was set up March 2 on Dorchester Heights, from which all of Boston could be shelled. Howe considered trying to take the Heights, but in the end decided he would not be able to with the troops he had. On February 7, he informed his officers that he had decided to save his army by evacuating the city. Over the next month, preparations were made for the evacuation by military and by Loyalists, many of whom preferred exile to remaining under the rebels. On March 17, the heavily-burdened fleet left Boston for Halifax. The next day, the city was occupied by the rebels.

## The Rebels Consolidate

Although the Canadian debacle was just becoming well known, the Congress had reasons to celebrate. In December 1775, Lord Dunmore had been forced to evacuate Norfolk, although he continued aboard ship to haunt Chesapeake Bay.

Early in 1776, Philip Schuyler and his troops had descended upon the estate of Sir John Johnson near Albany. A leading Tory and the King's agent for Indian Affairs, he not only possessed Iroquois allies but a number of Scots Catholic tenants. These were disarmed, and all of them forced to make their way in the dead of winter to Montreal, a journey which killed many of their women and children. Their priest, Fr. John Mckenna, reported to Bishop Briand all that had happened, while the men constituted themselves a regiment, the Royal Yorkers. Based at Ft. Niagara and led by Sir John, they vowed revenge on their former neighbors.

At last the need to employ the Loyalists had sunk in on

the cabinet in London. Since the bulk of Loyal strength in the Southern colonies lay inland, an elaborate plan was hatched by the British military as early as October 1775. A fleet from Cork, Ireland, would arrive off the coast of North Carolina. The Regulators and Scots Highlanders of the interior would rise, and make contact with the fleet. From there they would take South Carolina; Georgia would follow of its own accord. Then Lord Dunmore's friends in Virginia (and the black slaves he freed on condition that they fight for the Crown) would be supported in retaking that colony. The South would then serve as a base for the reclamation of the rest of the colonies.

But the fleet was delayed time and again. In February, the Highlanders and Regulators rose anyway. But on February 18 the little army was defeated at Moore's Creek Bridge. It was not until late Spring that the British fleet finally arrived. Finding their original landing place at Cape Fear unsuitable, they sailed south to Charleston. Here the guns at the mouth of the harbor drove them off. For the moment, the revolution was secure.

## The Declaration of Independence

From the beginning the rebels had protested their loyalty to their King, declaring that their quarrel was solely with his ministers. This was a situation which could not last. Early in 1776, *Thomas Paine*, a transplanted Englishman who had won Benjamin Franklin's favor prior to coming to America, wrote a pamphlet called *Common Sense*, in which he expressly charged the King with full responsibility for the war. More than this, he insulted George in language never before used of a King ("the Royal Brute"). Beyond this, he attacked the institution of Monarchy itself as "the Popery of government." From then on, radical propaganda advocating independence came out into the open.

The Continental Congress was made up of many different types of men, however. Many, such as George Washington, opposed independence: "I am as well satisfied as I can be of my existence that no such thing is desired by any thinking man in North America." But the military action which followed drove the most conservative delegates into the arms of the radicals.

In June, 1776, various of the Provincial Congresses began declaring their independence from Britain. On June 24, the Continental Congress declared that all colonists who adhered to or fought for Great Britain were guilty of treason and should be punished. Thomas Jefferson, perhaps the most talented writer among the Delegates, was set to writing a declaration of independence. This set down in forceful language that authority comes from the people, who have the right to alter or abolish their government, in accordance with the ideas of the Enlightenment. It then went on to describe the supposed crimes of King George III; how he had imposed taxes, incited the Indians, abolished English Law in a neighboring Province (Quebec), and so on. It is from this *Declaration of Independence* that most Americans today derive their views of George III.

When the Declaration was published in England, Thomas Hutchinson wrote a reply to it, based upon his experience as and information received while Royal governor of Massachusetts. In this pamphlet, he maintained that the cause of the struggle was not the "abuses and usurpations" of which the declaration accused King George, but the agitations of "men in each of the principal colonies who had independence in view before any of those taxes were laid or proposed which have since been the ostensible cause for resisting the execution of acts of Parliament." He maintained further that:

The tumults, riots, contempt and defiance of law in England were urged to encourage and justify the like disorders in the colonies and to annihilate the powers of government there. Many thousands of people who were before good and loyal subjects have been deluded and by degrees induced to rebel against the best of princes and the mildest of governments.

The Declaration, Hutchinson claimed, was intended "to reconcile the people of America to that Independence which always before they had been made to believe was not intended. This design has too well succeeded."

Whether Jefferson or Hutchinson was right, Congress passed the Declaration on July 2, 1776. Two days later, on July 4, it was signed. Ever since, this has been our national holiday, Independence Day. The flag was altered, 13 white stars on a blue field replacing the Union Jack in the corner. Church bells pealed throughout the colonies, and bonfires lit the night. There were cheers, parades, public speeches. The wooden image of the King in Baltimore was carted away and burned, while the statue of the King on horseback at New York's Bowling Green was pulled off its pedestal and taken to be melted. At Boston's Old State House and public buildings throughout America, the Royal Arms were hacked off or defaced. In the New England colonies, "King Street" in every town and village was renamed "State Street." With an Army, the Continental Congress, and now the Declaration, America seemed a real country at last.

## The Fall of New York

Immediately after the Declaration, things seemed to go well for the new nation. Tories and Indians in both South Carolina and Georgia were defeated.

But the British were not defeated. The first thing they required was a proper land base in the colonies. The obvious choice was the finest harbor in America, New York City. On August 22, they landed in Brooklyn from their base on Staten Island. Among these were Hessians, the first to be employed in the war. Guided by local Loyalists, the British and Hessians defeated the Americans on August 26, and after another battle at Brooklyn Heights, found themselves masters of Long Island. The Americans had withdrawn to New York City on the night of the 29th.

Interestingly enough, General Howe, commander of the British forces, was an outspoken member of the King's Whig opposition at home. He did nothing after the Americans withdrew for two weeks. Finally, on September 15, the British landed on Manhattan Island. The Americans withdrew from New York (at the time only covering the southern tip of Manhattan) and pulled back to Harlem Heights, where the next day they fought the British again. Howe once more made no further move, this time for a month.

At the other end of the colony, the remains of the American force sent to Canada had fallen back to Crown Point at the southern end of Lake Champlain. Over half of them were sick, when *General Horatio Gates* took command.

Back in Manhattan, Howe finally stirred on October 12. Outflanking the American positions, a strong force sailed up the Hudson river, landing at New Rochelle. Moving swiftly, the British and Hessians outmaneuvered and outfought the Americans, forcing Washington to abandon all of Southern Westchester County and the parts of New Jersey facing New York.

Then Washington and his men retreated across New Jersey, hotly pursued by the British. The Americans arrived in Newark on November 23 and left on the 28th; their pursuers arrived the same day. The day after that, Washington and his men passed through Brunswick, staying until December 1. Two days later, the British arrived. December 2 saw the

Continentals go through Princeton, where the British arrived five days later. The Americans having paused in Trenton on the 2nd, they rested until the 8th. Faced with capture by their opponents, they crossed over the Delaware River to Pennsylvania, abandoning most of New Jersey to the British. Then the news arrived that a British force of 6000 had occupied Newport, RI.

With New York firmly in British hands, and the Continental Army an exhausted, chilled, hungry band, it appeared to the British that the war was almost over, and that Christmas, 1776, would be a happy one for them. So too thought the Hessians guarding Trenton.

## Washington Crosses the Delaware

The American army was in a very bad position; the pursuit across New Jersey had not merely exhausted the troops and starved them. It had strained their morale so much that many deserted. An army which has suffered as much and has as little in the way of equipment as the Continentals did is generally on the way to defeat. But it was here that Washington's greatness as a leader became apparent.

It was one thing to command the army in Cambridge, when all that was needed was the conduct of a siege. Commanding a beaten force (particularly one as poorly organized as the Continentals were) and keeping it intact was quite different. But Washington rose to the occasion. He inspired his men in the midst of that dreary winter, despite the fact that many did not even have boots, but wrapped their feet in rags.

On Christmas Day, he led his men in a surprise move across the Delaware. The Hessians, still recovering from their Christmas Eve feasting, were completely unprepared. In 40 minutes without losing a single man, the Americans killed 22 and wounded 84 Hessians, taking the remaining 868 prisoner. It was one of the most complete victories ever gained by American soldiers.

General Howe allowed the Hessians to plunder New Jersey homes—whether rebel or Loyalist, indiscriminately. The result was to lose civilian support for the Royal cause. American counterattacks persuaded the British to withdraw from most of New Jersey by January 10, 1777. Washington's order to his men forbidding them to rob even Loyalists' houses did much to convert New Jersey to the Revolution.

In the meantime, Howe was once again delaying. Where would he strike? Would it be another attack from New York? An assault in the South?

In fact, the British had a much more complex plan. New England was the center of the revolt. Separate it from the other colonies, and they would sooner or later, given the large number of Loyalists in them and the Royal Navy's command of the sea, return to obedience. New England could then be reduced at leisure. To bring this about, General Howe would march north along the Hudson, Col. St. Leger would sweep along the Mohawk Valley, and *General John Burgoyne* would march south from Montreal. The three armies would meet at Albany, New York, and the plan would be accomplished.

Obviously, to be successful, all three commanders had to do their part. Unfortunately for the Royal cause, Howe once again decided to do something unexpected. In the short run, it appeared an easier and better target he aimed for; in the long run, it was disastrous. Leaving 9,000 troops in New York, he embarked 17,000 aboard ships bound for Chesapeake Bay. He had decided to attack Philadelphia, seat of the Congress.

## Failure of the Three Pronged Plan

On August 22, the British fleet appeared in the Chesa-

peake. They landed at Head of Elk, Maryland on the 25th.
After defeating the Americans at the Battle of Brandywine
Creek, Howe's troops made a slow and leisurely advance,
entering Philadelphia on September 27. As usual, Howe's
slow methods allowed many American troops to escape. The
Congress, having fled their capital, reconvened at York,
Pennsylvania.

Up North, the actions of the British were not as yet hampered by Howe's change of plans. The Americans evacuated
Ft. Ticonderoga without a shot on July 6. Burgoyne's column continued to advance, and the American defense of
Lake Champlain collapsed, as position after position was given
up without much struggle. By July 17, General Schuyler
had withdrawn his men all the way to Saratoga, while
Burgoyne marched steadily South. But on August 4, Schuyler
was replaced with General Horatio Gates.

During the same period, St. Leger advanced with his
Canadians, Indians, and Loyalists. Among the latter were Sir
John Johnson and his Royal Yorkers, accompanied by their
chaplain, Fr. John McKenna. By August 3, they had laid
siege to Ft. Stanwix, last major post on the road to Albany.

The Americans sent a column to relieve Ft. Stanwix that
same day. This was ambushed by Johnson's Royal Yorkers,
Col. John Butler's Queen's Rangers, and Chief Joseph Brant's
Mohawks. While the Loyalists and Indians were beaten off,
over half the rebels were killed, the remainder having to seek
refuge in the fort. Still, Oriskany is considered an American
victory. The siege continued sixteen more days, but the Loyalists' guns were too light to break down the fort's walls. Tir-
ing of this kind of warfare, most of the Mohawks left, forcing the Loyalists to end the siege and withdraw to their bases
in Canada. Thus neither the western nor the southern prong
of the invasion would be available to support Burgoyne.

The same day, a mostly Hessian detachment from

Burgoyne's army was defeated at Bennington, Vermont. Neither Bennington, Oriskany, nor the failure to take Ft. Stanwix boded well for Burgoyne. Worse, the further south he advanced, the farther his supplies had to travel from Lake Champlain.

On September 19, the British and Americans began the first battle at Saratoga. For almost a month the battle raged, but at last the Americans won. Overextended and undersupplied, Burgoyne surrendered with his 5791 remaining troops. This defeat, as we shall see, was the turning point of the war.

It did not seem so immediately, however. On October 4, Washington's attempt to drive Howe from Philadelphia failed at the battle of Germantown. Further attempts to dislodge the British failed, and in November the Americans withdrew to their Winter Quarters at Valley Forge. It was a hard winter, indeed. But in November, the Congress adopted a constitution for the new country, called *The Articles of Confederation.* Further, the rag tag army which camped out at Valley Forge received a drill master, *Baron von Steuben.* The traditions of the modern American army were started amid the snow of Valley Forge.

## The Beginning of the End

Philadelphia under the British was a town filled with celebrations. While the Continentals froze in Valley Forge, the Philadelphians enjoyed balls and all sorts of entertainments. This was the period when Major Clinton raised his Roman Catholic Volunteers from among the city's Catholics, to fight for the Crown.

But the home government refused to send Howe reinforcements. He sent in his resignation, and left in May 1778 for England. Once home, he took his seat in Parliament among the Whigs, and spent the rest of the war trying to bring down Lord North's Cabinet and defeat the King on the homefront.

He had certainly done his part in America. The Philadelphian adventure almost certainly insured the defeat at Saratoga, which bore fruit on February 8, 1778. King Louis XVI of France signed a treaty of trade and friendship with the United States, becoming the new nation's first ally. The effect in America was tremendous. Already, there were many French volunteers, such as the *Marquis de Lafayette*, serving with the Americans. In addition, there was a single regiment of French Canadians, Congress's Own Canadian Regiment, which had served at Saratoga. But this action of Louis XVI's served to legitimize the Congress for many. With French recognition, the United States no longer appeared to be merely a string of rebellious colonies. On March 13, the French government informed the British of their recognition of the United States, and a month later a fleet was sent out to America under the *Comte d'Estaing*.

Louis XVI committed his country to war with England for several reasons. France had fought and lost a long series of wars with England, which had cost the French much in men and money. Under King Louis, various reforms had been undertaken in the military which made victory seem possible. And Benjamin Franklin, American Ambassador at King Louis' court, had many friends in the French Government who added their pleas to Franklin's.

News of the coming French fleet impelled the British to withdraw from Philadelphia on June 10. Otherwise, they could have been bottled up in Chesapeake Bay. The French intervention changed the nature of the war completely. Britain and France were rivals not just in the West Indies, but in India and Africa as well. The Congress's attempts to win the French Canadians by conquest had failed, so too did their diplomatic mission in 1776. Before going to France, Franklin had gone to Quebec with Charles Carroll of Carrollton and his cousin, Fr. John Carroll. However charming the French court thought Franklin, their cousins in Canada did not. Bishop Briand (remembering the previous American actions) forbade any of his clergy to receive Fr. Carroll, and suspended one priest who did. But might not the French alliance change his and his people's mind?

At any rate, the British withdrew from Philadelphia across New Jersey, back toward New York. While on their way back, they were attacked with great losses at Monmouth Courthouse. At last, the British army, and the fleet which they had been afraid would be bottled up, arrived safely in New York on July 6. By the 11th, when the French fleet appeared off the New Jersey coast, there was nothing left for them to catch.

It was soon agreed between French and Americans that the British-held town of Newport, Rhode Island must be taken. D'Estaing set off for it, arriving offshore on July 29. The New England militia had been called to help in the siege. But on August 9 the British fleet arrived from New York. D'Estaing broke off the siege, and fought the British on the high sea. The French fleet was severely damaged, and sailed to Boston for repairs on August 24. Four days later, the commander of the American forces who had been besieging Newport from the land received news that the British fleet had returned to New York to bring reinforcements to Newport. The Americans withdrew.

The French ships had arrived in Boston in the meantime. Needing a place to say Mass, the French were assigned the Anglican church, King's Chapel. Having been the church of the Royal Governor before the war, it had lost most of its congregation after the evacuation. But the French dared not leave the Blessed Sacrament overnight in the church; the Bostonians, being fanatical anti-Catholics, would have desecrated it. So every day there was a procession from the French ships with the Host carried in a monstrance with incense, canopy, bell–all the signs of Popery the good Puritans of the town hated. The mob would line the street screaming abuse. Finally, on September 15, they attacked the procession, hoping to get at the Blessed Sacrament. But the *Chevalier de St. Sauveur*, a French officer, successfully defended it, being killed in the process. He was buried outside King's Chapel, where his monument may be seen today.

After this, relations between the French and Americans steadily improved in Boston, where a shocked reaction set in after the Chevalier's murder. On November 3, the French set sail for the West Indies, where they captured the islands of St. Vincent (June 16, 1779) and Grenada (July 4).

## Events in the West

The French Alliance and the Congress's recommendation to the states to seize all Loyalist property (to say nothing of increasing abuse of Loyalists in general) embittered those Tories who were under arms even more. On the frontier, those who had seen their children and wives perish in the winter of 1776 returned to burn and pillage with their Indian allies in the summer and autumn. Among these actions were the Cherry Valley and Wyoming Valley Massacres, where the Tories and Indians showed little mercy toward their rebel former neighbors. Westchester County, between the British lines north of New York City, and the American positions further north, became known as the "Neutral Ground." Irregular bands of Loyalists (called "Cowboys") and rebels vied with each other in cruelty and atrocities. Civil war is like that; for some reason, men are never as cruel to foreign foes as they are to their own people.

The Old Northwest (the present states of Ohio, Indiana, Illinois, Wisconsin, Michigan, and part of Minnesota) was mostly unsettled Indian country. Because the few posts

(Kaskaskia, Cahokia, Massac, Detroit, Green Bay, Michlimakinac, Ft. Chartres, Ft. Miami, Ft. St. Joseph, and Prairie du Chien) were inhabited by French settlers, the area had been made part of Quebec by the Quebec Act. All of these scattered settlements were served by a single, much-traveling priest, Fr. Pierre Gibault.

As a war measure, the British commander at Detroit, *Col. Henry Hamilton,* offered his Indian allies money for the scalps of rebel frontiersmen (hence his nickname, the "hairbuyer"). Apart from this annoyance, the whole area was claimed, on the basis of their Royal Charter, by the State of Virginia. The state authorities commissioned *George Rogers Clark* to conquer the Old Northwest for them. On July 4, 1778, he took Kaskaskia without firing a shot. There he met Fr. Gibault, whom he persuaded to join the American side. Cahokia fell bloodlessly also, and then, through Fr. Gibault, Vincennes. The Americans marched on, but Hamilton swept down from Detroit, and retook the town. However, a surprise attack by the Americans on February 23, 1779, forced Hamilton to surrender. Most of the Northwest was now in American hands. As for Fr. Gibault, he reconsidered his actions after the war ended, and Protestant settlers began to pour in. "I always regretted and do regret every day the loss of the mildness of British rule," he said, considering what the exchange of the Quebec Act for the Articles of Confederation really meant.

The summer of 1779 was spent by American forces devastating the land of the Iroquois in New York. By September, the land of the Six Nations was burned out, the Iroquois themselves were dependent on British handouts, and the frontier was freed of Indian terror.

## The War Drags On

New York remained under British occupation a bustling

port. It was a center of Loyalism, as Tories from Continental-held areas sought refuge there. A number of Loyalist regiments were quartered there, one of which was the Catholic Volunteers of Ireland, led by Lord Rawdon. On March 17, 1779, they held the first St. Patrick's Day Parade, at which was sung this song:

> Success to the shamrock, and all those who wear it;
> Be honor their portion wherever they go.
> May riches attend them and stores of good claret,
> For how to employ them sure none better know.
> Every foe surveys them with terror,
> But every silk petticoat wishes them nearer.
> So Yankee keep off or you'll soon learn your error,
> For Paddy shall prostrate lay every foe.
> This day, but the year I can't rightly determine,
> Saint Patrick the vipers did chase from the land.
> Let's see if like him we can't sweep off the vermin,
> Who dare 'gainst the sons of the shamrock to stand.
> Hand in hand! Let's carol the chorus,
> As long as the blessings of Ireland hang o'er us,
> The crest of rebellion shall tremble before us,
> Like brothers while thus we march hand in hand.

In December of 1778, the British had taken Savannah, which was immediately reinforced by a column from the British garrison at St. Augustine, Florida. Within a few months, most of Georgia was in the hands of Loyalists. Such American forces as remained in the State were too weak to retake it.

The next step was the invasion of South Carolina. Moving rapidly, British troops reached Charleston on May 8, and three days later demanded the city's surrender. In return, the State government replied that if the British would withdraw from South Carolina, they would become neutral, and go with the winning side after the war. The British commander refused, and the siege began. But a determined defense, partly commanded by the Polish officer *Casimir Pulaski,* led the British to call off the attack. They withdrew to Georgia in June.

That same month, Louis XVI's cousin, Charles III of Spain, also declared war on England and immediately began besieging the British naval base of Gibraltar. On August 16, a combined French and Spanish fleet arrived off Plymouth, England; all the while, *Admiral John Paul Jones* was sinking British ships wherever he found them in British waters. Although the Allied fleet was called off from Plymouth, it showed the erosion of British naval power—the country's main strength—in this war.

This had repercussions in America. Not only did the British evacuate Newport, D'Estaing had returned to American waters after his victories in the West Indies. The plan was to attack the British at Savannah from both land and sea. On September 8, the French fleet arrived off Savannah. By the 16th, the city was surrounded by land. It was not until October 3, however, that the cannon were emplaced. News came that a British fleet was on its way to relieve the city; the Americans and French stormed Savannah on October 9. It was a complete failure—and Pulaski was killed.

It mattered little to the Americans that the Spanish Governor of Louisiana, Bernardo de Galvez, had spent the summer conquering Baton Rouge and Natchez from the British, with a mixed force of Spanish, Irish, Cajuns, and Mexicans.

## Victory from Defeat

Never had American fortunes seemed at such a low ebb. In the immediate, things were to get worse. Because the new nation had no coinage, and its paper money was soon worthless, keeping the army supplied was difficult, despite French and Spanish aid, and the latter's conquest of Mobile on January 10, 1780. In the North, Washington was kept pinned around New York; the defeat at Savannah and the departure of the French Navy left the South at the mercy of the British and Loyalists, who had become the bulk of the Crown's forces there.

Howe's successor, **Sir Henry Clinton** decided to take Charleston at last. Borne by ship from New York, the British landed near Charleston on March 29, and began their siege in early April. The British fleet cut off the city from any hope of rescue, since D'Estaing was nowhere near. Finally, on May 9 Charleston, with the only regular American army in the South, surrendered.

The long war had produced many strains in England itself. 1779 had been a very bad year for the Crown, considering all the defeats and difficulties. The King's enemies in Parliament were clamoring for both an end to the war and to the King's personal rule through Lord North. Meetings were held throughout the land, and Britain was near bankruptcy. Things reached the boiling point in June, 1780 when Lord George Gordon, an apostate Catholic, led the London mob in rioting in an attempt to bring down the King and his cabinet. After burning Catholic chapels, setting fire to Newgate Prison and attacking the Bank of England, the rioters attempted to storm the House of Commons.

George III reacted quickly. Troops were dispatched to London, and 450 rioters killed or wounded. Shortly after calm was restored, news of the victory at Charleston arrived. For the moment, the war would continue. Yet it could not last forever. A large French army under *General Jean Baptiste de Rochambeau* arrived at Newport on July 12, 1780.

In the South, the struggle between Tories and rebels became ever bloodier. Atrocities were committed on both sides as they became increasingly embittered toward one another. It was guerrilla warfare, of a type that the world has come to know all too well since.

Apart from these struggles, 1780 passed into 1781 without any more major campaigns in North America. In the West Indies, Senegal and the Guinea Coast, and particularly in India, France and Spain fought Great Britain on a similar scale to the fighting in North America. In early 1781, the Netherlands joined France and Spain, and promptly began losing West Indian, African, and Indian possessions to the British.

The British commander in the South, *Lord Cornwallis*, was concerned to finally conquer the area, once and for all. The remaining American forces, under *General Daniel Morgan* received their supplies from Virginia. Cornwallis resolved to cut Morgan's supply lines, deciding to invade North Carolina. But on January 17, at a decisive battle called the Cowpens, his light cavalry were destroyed. This was disastrous, because the Americans decided to lure the British after them in typical guerrilla fashion; if they could avoid being defeated, they could wear the British down. Without light cavalry, it was doubtful if Cornwallis' troops would be able to catch up with the Americans.

A second problem was that the invasion of North Carolina was done without alerting the resident Loyalists in time. This blunder meant that much in the way of intelligence and the recruiting of more light troops was not done. At any rate, Cornwallis pursued the Americans toward Virginia for months, inflicting a defeat on them at Guilford Courthouse, where his own losses were nevertheless very heavy. Afterwards, Cornwallis retreated south along the Cape Fear River to Wilmington to recover at a seaport where the Royal Navy could supply his exhausted forces. The Americans he had been pursuing returned to South Carolina to begin seizing the British posts outside of Charleston.

Cornwallis left Wilmington, reaching Virginia in early

May. Plantation rich, the State seemed to offer unlimited spoils, and the British lost no time in taking them. There were few troops capable of resisting Cornwallis' army; more and more the campaign became an affair of pure plunder. Washington decided to move his own and Rochambeau's armies south; similarly, the French Admiral De Grasse moved his ships toward Chesapeake Bay.

To avoid a pitched encounter with these armies, Cornwallis moved his army to Yorktown in early September. Strategically placed on a peninsula, it offered a secure haven to await a British fleet and be evacuated. Of course, the plan depended on British control of the sea. But on September 5, De Grasse defeated and drove off the British fleet. The trap was sprung, and Cornwallis' troops were under siege, surrendering on October 17. The surrender ceremony was serenaded by the Scots bagpipers playing a funeral dirge, *The World Turned Upside Down*. Afterwards, those officers of the British, French, and American armies who happened to be Freemasons held a banquet together. For all practical purposes, the loss of Cornwallis' large army doomed the British land effort in North America. A few weeks afterwards, the French recaptured from the British the Dutch island of St. Eustatius in the West Indies, with the sum of £2,000,000.

The summer had seen the increasingly outnumbered Loyalists and British swept out of the interior of South Carolina. On September 8, 1781, at the battle of Eutaw Springs, the last pitched battle of the war was fought. The British won, but withdrew to Charleston; they were not in a position to follow up their victory. Shortly afterward, they evacuated Wilmington.

In London, news of Yorktown and St. Eustatius was a heavy blow to Lord North's cabinet. In February, 1782, the Whigs had gathered enough strength in Parliament to "authorize" (in reality, to order) the King to seek a truce with the Americans. Soon after this, the Island of Minorca in the Mediterranean fell to the French and Spanish, and word arrived of the fall of the British West Indian islands of St. Kitt's, Nevis, and Montserrat. Lord North's government could not survive these disasters. He resigned on March 20, and a Whig cabinet, filled with the King's enemies, came to power. The new Prime Minister, Rockingham, informed George III that peace with the colonies must be made, even if it meant independence. The war was over, although the treaty was not signed until 1783. A new nation had been born.

## THE RESULTS

Why did the British lose? First, because they did not understand the nature of the threat posed by the pro-independence leaders; the warnings of men like Hutchinson were ignored. Second, because they did not attempt to organize Loyalists in the way the Committees of Correspondence and Sons of Liberty were organized. Third, because of the poor generalship of Sir William Howe. Fourth, because of the intervention of France and Spain.

The first result of the Revolution was, with the evacuation by the British of Savannah, Charleston, and finally New York, the exile of those Loyalists—about 100,000 or so—who could not reconcile themselves to the new regime. Many went to Ontario, New Brunswick, Nova Scotia, and the "Eastern Townships" of Quebec; these were the founders of English-speaking Canada. Many others went to the Bahamas, Bermuda, Barbados, Jamaica, and other West Indian islands. In the first named, they were as influential as they were in Canada. Still others went to England. But the original 13 States lost much by this emigration. Other Loyalists (like St. Elizabeth Anne Seton's family and in-laws) stayed, making the best they could of things.

George III's attempt to restore his country's constitution was ruined, the Whigs returned to cabinet, and the oligarchy regained control of power in Great Britain, which they have held ever since. Further, due to the war with France and Spain, and the activities of the Carrolls and other Catholic leaders in the colonies, the King became opposed to Catholic Emancipation. This would serve in time to alienate most of the Catholic Irish from the throne forever.

France had won—but was bankrupt. The French received little from their share of the war, except an enormous debt and a great many noblemen who served in the army in America infected with dangerous ideas. Yet the war had proved Louis XVI's abilities as a wartime leader. To him, more than any other one man, might be given the credit for the independence of the United States. In return, he would find his own crown threatened a mere six years after the peace treaty.

The Spanish received Florida, and a claim to a good part more of the American West—Mississippi, Alabama, and Tennessee. They would soon find themselves in friction with the country they had helped create.

America now had a legal existence as a country. But only the slightest framework of nationhood was present as yet, although an American nationality had begun to emerge during the war years. The States were considered the important units of the country. National borders were still in dispute, and the Indians in the unorganized territories of the Old Southwest and Northwest still were allied to Spain and Britain. National life still remained to be defined. We will see that definition in the next chapter.

---

See Appendix I on p.181 for a list of Loyalist Sites.

# THE
# YOUNG
# NATION
# 1783-1815

## AT THE BEGINNING

The end of the year 1783 saw a new nation universally recognized among the countries of the world: the United States of America. Where the seat of sovereignty in the British Empire had been, on the surface, the King, in the United States matters were not so clear. For on declaring themselves independent states, the state governments considered themselves to have taken the place of George III. This meant that the Continental Congress was no more than a gathering place for emissaries from such regimes, rather than a sovereign body in its own right.

Every revolution is fought for two reasons: the declared reason, usually having to do with freedom in the abstract; and the real reason, involving merely the transference of power from one group to another. More of the revolutionaries are interested in the first than the second reason, but it is generally the leadership which is concerned with the latter.

So it was with our revolution. Many of the idealistic had joined it thinking that "freedom" from the Crown would mean the freedom of each state to do as it pleased—the states after all being more answerable to their people than a large federal government would be. For such folk, authority came, not from God, as all Christian countries at that time claimed, but from the people themselves. But where a King is an individual, and may be held accountable for his wielding of God's authority, the people are too numerous to be responsible for anything. Further, since their desires rather than God's are to be the standard against which all must be judged, anything the majority appears to wish must be good. Naturally, since it is physically impossible for all the people to man the positions of governance, their powers must be used on their behalf. Those who actually do so are perforce the real rulers of the land. -

So it was and so it is in this country. But with the states as the real powers under *The Articles of Confederation* (as the first constitution was called), this was a much more difficult affair. While it is true that the local oligarchy in each state had taken complete power during the revolution, they tended to be extremely limited in their worldview; less interested in spreading the doctrines of the American Revolution around the world than in making a profit at home. But for the more ideologically motivated among them this was not enough. Massachusetts was too small for John Adams, Pennsylvania for Franklin, Virginia for Jefferson, and so on. For such as these, it was not enough to have a string of little countries hugging the Atlantic coast: they wished to lay the foundations of a great commonwealth which, dedicated to the principles of the Enlightenment and Freemasonry, would serve as model for and steppingstone to a world state based upon the same ideals. For such as these, the American was to be a new kind of man. Like their Puritan predecessors, who had wished to sever themselves completely from Catholicism, they wished to cut off all connection to old Europe and to the revealed religion which had formed her. We shall look more closely at this presently.

But in 1783, the material at hand did not look very promising. The Articles safeguarded the powers of the states carefully. Although each of them could have from two to seven representatives at Congress, the states had no more than one vote apiece, in the unicameral body. There was no chief executive to administer and execute laws passed: the President of the Congress was no more than an official charged with enforcing parliamentary procedure, like today's Speaker of the House. Neither was there any national court system, each state's judiciary being completely independent. Nine out of the thirteen states had to agree for a bill to become law, and Congress could neither levy taxes nor tariffs. It could not regulate commerce, and so each state could (and did) tax goods coming in from the next state (this was particularly hard on the New Jersey farmers; those in the north traded in New York City, and those in the south in Philadelphia. They described their state as "a barrel tapped at both ends"). All the states had to consent to amending the Articles, which were in any case merely a "firm league of friendship" among the states, rather than basic law.

Had all 13 states been identical in economic interests, social structure, and ethnic make-up, such a legal arrangement alone would have been a fertile source of difficulty and dissension. But they were far from identical.

## State of the Union

New England had been the starting point of the revolution. Men like turncoat Royal Governor Jonathan Trumbull, John Hancock, Sam Adams, Paul Revere, and of course, John Adams continued to play an important part in local affairs, serving as assemblymen, governors, and the like. Massachusetts, Connecticut, and New Hampshire were dominated by the same groups of urban merchants and bureaucrats who had been the mainstay of power under the Crown (although many individuals of these classes–including a large number of Harvard and Yale alumni–had fled to Canada as Loyalists). Correspondingly, many of the rural inhabitants of these states, no longer having a Royal Governor to appeal to, found themselves over-taxed and foreclosed upon by the same men they had helped to bring to complete power in the recent conflict. The Vermont farmers, whose lands were still disputed by New Hampshire and New York, simply carried on as an independent country, not recognizing and unrecognized by the Congress.

Although the New Englanders were ethnically homogenous–British Isles with a little French Huguenot, like the Reveres–they had religious tensions. In Massachusetts, the Congregational remained the State Church. Article III of the Commonwealth's 1780 constitution declared that:

> ...the happiness of a people, and the good order and preservation of civil government, essentially depend upon piety, religion, and morality; and...these cannot be generally diffused through a community but by the institution of the public worship of God, and of public instructions in piety, religion, and morality.

To this end, the same article gave the legislature the right to make the towns of the Commonwealth levy taxes to support "public protestant teachers of piety, religion, and morality," these latter being the Congregational ministers.

But while this establishment (which endured until 1833) was essentially the same which had prevailed before the revolution, it had a very different end in mind from that of the Puritan fathers. They had made theirs the state church to safeguard what they thought was Christianity; their descendants retained the arrangement to protect the civil order. This was a reflection of the decline of belief in the doctrines of the Congregational religion, and the corresponding growth of what would later be called Unitarianism. Even so, the established church was opposed by the Baptists, who were the largest religious minority in the Commonwealth. Yet both united in maintaining Test Acts which excluded Catholics from public office (although, in view of the contributions of France and Spain, they were graciously allowed to exist). Yet some were annoyed by this last liberality; the Town Meeting of Dunstable, for example, called upon the legislature to deny "Protection to the Idolatrous worshippers of the Church of Rome."

Connecticut and New Hampshire also retained establishments like Massachusetts, as well as Test Acts. The Republic of Vermont, while not having a State Church, nevertheless required its office-holders to believe in God, the Old and New Testaments, and the Protestant religion. Rhode Island's status quo merely continued.

The Middle States were quite different. New York, with its cosmopolitan population, and Pennsylvania and Delaware with their large German minorities, were dominated by an urban merchant class in New York City and Philadelphia, and by great landed estate holders. In New York, for example, while Loyalist Patroons like the De Lanceys had been forced out, the rebel Van Rensselaers, the Livingstons, the Gardiners and others continued to rule their manors as they had for generations. New Jersey was still the domain of her British, Dutch, and German small farmers. In Delaware, New Jersey, and Pennsylvania, as no religion had been established prior to the revolution, neither was any afterwards. But the latter's 1776 constitution did require office-holders to believe in God and the Old and New Testaments—thus excluding Jews. Franklin among others led a drive on their behalf, and in 1790 this was amended to belief in God and "a future state of rewards and punishments."

New York was significantly different from these other states in two ways. First, that in the southern four counties the Anglican Church had been established, which state of affairs was ended in the state's 1777 constitution. Second, that specific opposition to Catholicism, lead by such American heroes as William Livingston and John Jay, was particularly vicious. Jay's Party advocated exiling all Catholics. Having failed in this, they were able to obtain in 1788 a Test Oath requiring that all officeholders renounce all foreign powers "ecclesiastical as well as civil." This prevented Catholics from holding office there.

Where New England depended heavily on shipping and the slave trade, and the Mid-Atlantic looked to both trade and agriculture, the South was overwhelmingly rural; except for North Carolina, these states were dominated by the plantations. The mountaineers and small farmers continued to resent the great landholders as they had before the revolution. Germans were found in the Piedmont of Virginia and Maryland, in the interior of South Carolina, and in ports like Charleston, Baltimore, and Savannah; Scots Highlanders (many speaking Gaelic) could be met in the New Scotland area of North Carolina, and Georgia's Darien settlement; and Ulster Scots prevailed in the Hill Country. But with these exceptions, as well as Charleston's Huguenots, most Southern whites were of English descent.

Thus, the Church of England was established in all these states at the beginning of the revolution. In 1784, the Virginia assembly transformed this into a requirement that all Virginians be taxed, not for the support of the Episcopal Church, but for the Christian denomination of their choice—as is done in Germany today. Unrelenting propaganda by the Deists in the Assembly however, brought about the passage two years later of Jefferson's Act for Establishing Religious Freedom, which severed all connection between the government of the Commonwealth of Virginia and any religious body.

South Carolina's 1778 constitution established "Protestantism" as the state religion, and barred all non-protestants from public office. Thus, in addition to the Anglican-Episcopal Church, Baptists, Presbyterians, Independent Calvinists (Congregationalists), and Methodists were all registered as established churches. In 1790, the state's new constitution abolished all mention of church establishment, and ordered the "free exercise and enjoyment of religious profession and worship, without discrimination or preference." North Carolina's 1776 constitution ended the establishment of the Episcopal Church as well, frankly forbidding establishment of any church; but offices were restricted to Protestants and remained so well into the 19th century. Georgia's 1777 constitution was similar. Maryland, however, while opening offices to all Christians in 1776, retained the Episcopal Church as the established one, with all provisions giving the state control of it to remain in force—except for funding. It was not until 1810 that the last vestige of establishment was abolished. Only Christians could hold office until the early 19th century, and office-holders were still required to believe in God until the 1950's.

The states had abdicated their claims to the western lands in favor of Congress. But in 1783, Congress had no troops of its own to patrol the frontier, a job left to the militias. The result was that both Great Britain and Spain felt no need to recognize American sovereignty in large parts of the Old Northwest and Old Southwest. The British continued to occupy posts at Michilimakinac, Detroit, Niagara, Oswego, and elsewhere. These posts both kept order, functioned as trading posts, and acted as liaison points with the Indian tribes of the area, who retained their attachment to George III despite being within American jurisdiction, even as their fathers had two decades before attempted to maintain their loyalty to Louis XV after the British victory.

Spain, meanwhile, had a legitimate complaint against the United States. Under British rule, the northern border of West Florida had been extended considerably. In a secret agreement, the Americans agreed to the British retaining the new boundary, should they regain the province at the peace table (Spain having conquered it during the Revolution). The Spanish, however, both kept West Florida, and later learned of the agreement. They then claimed the wider borders for their own. Large tribes of the area, such as the Creek, Choctaw, and Chickasaw allied with the Spanish.

But nevertheless, American penetration continued. In Ohio, Kentucky, and Tennessee, in particular, large numbers settled. The French settlers of the old posts of Vincennes, Kaskaskia, and Cahokia found themselves joined by many of the newcomers, who would eventually outnumber them. As might be supposed, neither they nor their Indian neighbors were pleased by this prospect.

This, then, was the state of the new nation at the commencement of its career.

## The Faith of the Founding Fathers

Despite the apparently ramshackle nature of the country, those who had been its ideological mentors in the revolution—some of whom (Adams, Jefferson, and Madison) would later preside over it—had great plans for it. It would be, as we have said, a country based not upon any sort of Christianity, but upon the ideals of the Enlightenment. This is a statement which will shock some, and so it is well to quote Franklin, Jefferson, and Adams on religion, so as to make the position of the most important of the founders clear.

A few weeks before he died, Benjamin Franklin wrote a letter to Yale's president, Ezra Stiles:

> Here is my creed. I believe in one God, Creator of the Universe. That he governs it by His providence. That He ought to be worshipped. That the most acceptable service we render Him is doing good to his other children. That the soul of man is immortal, and will be treated with justice in another life respecting its conduct in this. As to Jesus of Nazareth, my opinion of whom you particularly desire, I think the system of morals and his religion, as he left them to us, the best the world ever saw or is likely to see; but I apprehend it has received various corrupt changes, and I have, with most of the dissenters in England, some doubts as to his divinity; though it is a question I do not dogmatize upon, having never studied it, and think it needless to busy myself with it now, when I expect soon an opportunity of knowing the truth with less trouble. I see no harm, however, in its being believed, if that belief has the good consequence, as it probably has, of making his doctrines more respected and better observed...

This is a classic statement of Deism. The God of whom Franklin writes is not the Christian God, Whose Second Person incarnates of a Virgin and remains in Church and Sacraments. Rather, he is the Muslim Allah or the Masonic Grand Architect, essentially aloof from his creation. Revealed Christianity is spurious, but serves a useful social function. This last, essentially dishonest notion, led many of Franklin's co-theorists to support the Congregational establishment in New England. It is astonishing that Franklin never studied the question of Christ's divinity, especially when he had spent so much time with his friend, Fr. John Carroll—particularly when they went together to Canada to attempt to seduce the French there from their allegiance to the King. One assumes they had other things to speak of during their long acquaintance.

Where Franklin, however, saw in Christianity merely a harmless, perhaps even useful lie, Jefferson saw a definite evil. As he wrote to Mrs. Harrison Smith on August 6, 1816:

> My opinion is that there would never have been an infidel if there had never been a priest. The artificial structures they have built on the purest of all moral systems, for the purpose of deriving from it pence and power, revolts those who think for themselves, and who read in the system only what is really there.

But he saw signs of hope in the country which he both helped to create and which he ruled over for a time. To it, in a letter of June 26, 1822 for Benjamin Waterhouse, he imputed a messianic mission:

> I rejoice that in this blessed country of free inquiry and belief, which has surrendered its creed and conscience to neither Kings nor priests, the genuine doctrine of one only God is reviving, and I trust that there is not a *young man* now living in the United States who will not die a Unitarian.

Thus spake the author of the Declaration of Independence, who even wrote his own "de-mythologized" version of the Bible to prove his point. While he and John Adams had been intense political opponents in office, their shared religious opinions served as a means of reconciliation in retirement. Their correspondence has been preserved; the intriguing thing about it all is that where Jefferson was the more radical politically, in religious matters it is Adams who appears in the correspondence as the more bitter opponent of Christianity, and of Catholicism in particular.

On December 3, 1813, Adams informed Jefferson that:

> Indeed, Mr. Jefferson, what could be invented to de-
> base the ancient Christianism, which Greeks, Romans,
> Hebrews, and Christian factions, above all the Catho-
> lics, have not fraudulently imposed upon the public?
> Miracles after miracles have rolled down in torrents, wave
> succeeding wave in the Catholic Church, from the Coun-
> cil of Nice, and long before, to this day.

In the same letter, he goes on to describe a book of
Chateaubriand's (which he nevertheless admitted to reading
"with delight") as "enthusiastic, bigoted, superstitious, Roman Catholic throughout." He saw an innate conflict between his and Jefferson's religion, and Catholicism, as he
wrote to Jefferson on July 16, 1814:

> If the Christian religion, as I understand it, or as you
> understand it, should maintain its ground, as I believe it
> will, yet Platonic, Pythagoric, Hindoo, and cabalistical
> Christianity, which is Catholic Christianity, and which
> has prevailed for fifteen hundred years, has received a
> mortal wound, of which the monster must finally die.

And again on June 20, 1815:

> The question before the human race is, whether the
> God of Nature shall govern the world by his own laws,
> or whether the priests and kings shall rule it by fictitious
> miracles? Or, in other words, whether authority is origi-
> nally in the people? Or whether it has descended for 1800
> years in a succession of popes and bishops, or brought
> down from heaven by the Holy Ghost in the form of a
> dove, in a phial of holy oil? [This latter refers to a miracle
> which occurred at the coronation of Clovis, King of the
> Franks.]

February 2, 1816 finds him referring to "that stupendous
monument of human hypocrisy and fanaticism, the church

of St. Peter at Rome..." (Presumably he had no such opinion about the public buildings in Washington, such as the Capitol and White House, first used in his administration).

The principal author of the constitution, James Madison, wrote to a Reverend Adams in 1832 that: "In the Papal System, Government and Religion are in a manner consolidated, and that is found to be the worst of Government."

These sentiments required for their practical execution the creation of a distinct American character, made-to-order rather than organically developed over long centuries influenced by the Faith, as happened in Europe. There must be, in as many ways as possible, a radical divorce from both the mother country and the rest of Old Europe. Foremost in the pursuance of this goal was *Noah Webster*, famous as the creator of *Webster's Dictionary of the American Language*. The very name of the book tells us something about his intentions in altering the spelling of such words as honour, centre, and recognise to honor, center, and recognize. This change he called a "reform." In a 1789 essay he justified it on several grounds, but the one which most concerned him was simply that it "would make a difference between the English orthography and the American....I am confident that such an event is an object of vast political consequence." What was his goal?

> ...a *national language* is a bond of *national union*. Every engine should be employed to render the people of this country truly *national;* to call their attachments home to their own country; and to inspire them with the pride of national character. However they may boast of independence, and the freedom of their government, yet their *opinions* are not sufficiently independent; an astonishing respect for the arts and literature of their parent country and a blind imitation of its manners are still prevalent among the Americans.

Webster's efforts in this area soon received official commendation, and eventually prevailed. Here he realized a fact grasped by later revolutionaries: if all traces of the old regime are to be blotted out, the language and its manner of writing must themselves be changed. So Kemal Ataturk ordered Turkish to be written in Latin rather than Arabic letters; the Soviets "reformed" the Russian alphabet; and Mao had the Chinese characters "simplified." The result was to make their nations' literatures difficult or impossible for the younger generations to read, in hopes of cutting them off from affection for the former state of their lands. It was an extension of this principle which led George Orwell to his horrific vision of "Newspeak" in *1984*.

But Webster and his kind were not merely concerned with how things were spelled. They were also concerned with rejecting the inheritance of Christendom in education. In another essay, written in 1790, Webster argued for the banishing of classical and British literature from classrooms, and for their replacement with something else:

> Another defect in our schools, which, since the Revolution, is become inexcusable, is the want of proper books. The collections which are now used consist of essays that respect foreign and ancient nations. The minds of youth are perpetually led to the history of Greece and Rome or to Great Britain; boys are constantly repeating the acclamations of Demosthenes and Cicero or debates upon some political question in the British Parliament...
>
> But every child in America should be acquainted with his own country....As soon as he opens his lips, he should rehearse the history of his own country; he should lisp the praise of liberty and of those illustrious heroes and statesmen who have wrought a revolution in her favor.

In a word, education ought not to be the expansion of the mind so as to assist both in life and salvation, but at base, ideological indoctrination. Rather than teach the student, via the great minds of Western Civilization, how to think (and so evaluate things himself) he was to be initiated into the sort of nation-worship which was then being formulated, but which has been the mainstay of education in this country ever since.

It has been said that the public schools have been one of the major instruments of assimilation in this country. Indeed they have been, for their job has been precisely that outlined by Webster. They have insured that the basic ideas of the Enlightenment (as held by Franklin, Jefferson, and company) so opposed to Christianity in general and Catholicism in particular, became and remain the basic intellectual currency of this country. We will now see the response of the Catholic Church to this.

## The Founding of Americanist Catholicism

The Catholic minority, centered as it was in Maryland, Pennsylvania, and Delaware, could not help but be affected by their country's independence. Prior to the war, American Catholics had been under the remote jurisdiction of the Vicar Apostolic of London, and served in large part by ex-Jesuits. The Vicar Apostolic himself (as with the Irish bishops and the Scots and other English Vicars Apostolic) was chosen by the Pope usually on the advice of the Cardinal-Duke of York, Henry Stuart. Brother of Bonnie Prince Charlie (Charles III, according to the Jacobites; his brother would inherit his claims in 1788, and would be called Henry IX afterwards), he was the highest-ranking English-speaking prelate. Would he not be consulted on the appointment of an American bishop, now that the States were a separate country?

No. Although Fr. Carroll had not apparently discussed the divinity of Christ with Franklin on their Quebec trip, he had made himself useful in other ways. Already aged, Franklin wrote on the trip that "I find I grow daily more feeble, and I think I could hardly have got so far but for Mr. Carroll's friendly assistance and care for me." Here we see a pattern which has dominated the Church in America from that day to this—practice of the corporal works of mercy to the exclusion of the spiritual.

At any rate, although Carroll had kept himself aloof from his brother priests after his return from Europe (where he was educated and ordained) in 1774, his brother Daniel's and cousin Charles of Carrollton's prominent positions as revolutionaries won him the appointment to the Canadian mission. With theirs and Franklin's continued support, he became afterwards *de facto* head of the body of priests functioning in America. This was made official in 1784. Franklin's journal for July 1 of that year has these words: "The Pope's Nuncio called and acquainted me that the Pope had, *on my recommendation*, appointed Mr. John Carroll superior of the Catholic clergy in America, with many powers of a bishop; and that, probably he would be made bishop *in partibus* before the end of the year." Franklin's view of his part in the affair is confirmed by the letter of appointment sent to Carroll himself, wherein Cardinal Antonelli writes:

> ...it is known that your appointment will please and gratify many members of that republic, and especially Mr. Franklin, the eminent individual who represents that republic at the court of the Most Christian King.

So rather than depending on a holy Cardinal who had forfeited a temporal kingdom for the sake of his vocation, the choice of first bishop of this nation was made by a man who did not believe in the divinity of Christ.

But what sort of beliefs did Carroll have regarding the Faith? He considered two great problems in the Church of his time to be "the boundaries of the spiritual jurisdiction of the Holy See," and "the use of the Latin tongue in the publick Liturgy." On these he wrote to Fr. Joseph Berington in 1787:

> I consider these two points as the greatest obstacles to Christians of other denominations to a thorough union with us, or at least to a much more general diffusion of our religion, particularly in N. America....With respect to the latter point, I cannot help thinking that the alteration of the Church discipline ought not only to be solicited, but insisted upon as essential to the service of God and benefit of mankind. Can there be anything more preposterous than an unknown tongue; and in this country either for want of books or inability to read, the great part of our congregations must be utterly ignorant of the meaning and sense of the publick office of the Church.

As to the former point, Carroll had made himself very clear prior to his appointment as head of the clergy, in an April 10, 1784 letter to Fr. Plowden:

> ...that no authority derived from the Propaganda will ever be admitted here; that the Catholick Clergy and Laity here know that the only connexion they ought to have with Rome is to acknowledge the Pope as Spiritual head of the Church; that no Congregations existing in his States shall be allowed to exercise any share of his Spiritual authority here; that no Bishop Vicar Apostolical shall be admitted, and if we are to have a Bishop, he shall not be in partibus (a refined Roman political contrivance), but an ordinary national Bishop, in whose appointment Rome shall have no share; so that we are very easy about their machinations.

From such sentiments, it may even be inferred that had Rome not given him the appointment later that year, he might even have formed his own schismatic church. In any case, it is obvious that he wished not only a vernacular liturgy but the Pope reduced to the position of the Anglican Archbishop of Canterbury—in a word, that the Catholic Church in America should be an imitation of the Episcopal church. Today, he seems to have obtained his wish.

But what was this worthy prelate's stance on conversions, which, in a non-Catholic country like this one, is presumably the clergy's first interest? An answer may be found in his famed prayer for the Civil Authorities. After praying for the deliberations and conduct of the President, Congress, and so forth, the following paragraph is recited:

> We recommend likewise, to Thy unbounded mercy, all our brethren and fellow-citizens throughout the United States, that they may be blessed and sanctified in the observance of Thy most holy law; that they may be preserved in union, and in that peace which the world cannot give; and after the blessings of this life, be admitted to those which are eternal.

There is here no mention of conversion, or indeed of anything spiritual, save observance of the Divine Law. This is redolent of the sort of moralistic Deism which we saw promulgated by the Founding Fathers. Franklin himself could have recited it in good conscience. In place of the salvation offered by the Church's sacraments we seem to see here a temporal one envisaged. What is this union in which Americans must be preserved? It is not one of faith, obviously.

Yet herein was established the attitude towards conversion of America which has prevailed in the US Church until the present: that the country does not need to be converted at all, because in some mysterious way it is already joined to the Church.

## Problems of Confederation

The Congress being ineffective, jurisdictional bickering broke out between the states continually, such as that between New York and New Jersey over operation of a light house at Sandy Hook. Spanish, Indian, and British activity against American settlement could not be countered for lack of a standing army. No national coinage meant that the country had to rely on worthless paper notes and a dizzying array of French, Spanish, British, and other foreign coins.

This last was symbolic of the country's economy as a whole. Unable to levy taxes, the only way Congress could operate (let alone repay the debts incurred during the revolution) was to either borrow yet more money or ask the states to contribute—voluntarily, of course. Foreign nations would not negotiate over trade with Congress because each state had its own tariff policy. Despite the high hopes held for the new nation by the ideologues, the future did not look bright.

Within three years after the treaty, signs of impending ruin began to make themselves felt. Desperate for money, the Congress leased control of both shores of the Mississippi to Spain for a period of 25 years in 1786. While the needed gold and silver did help shore up the country's rocky finances, it was a terrible blow to national pride.

New England began to show signs of severe instability. Thus in 1786 a band of New Hampshire farmers marched on their state capital to demand lowering of their taxes and issuance of more paper money. Massachusetts was rocked by Shays's Rebellion. Bunker Hill veteran **Daniel Shays** led a band of farmers in the western part of the Commonwealth, who protested the lack of real money, high interest rates, widespread foreclosures, and a taxation rate which unfairly placed the greater part of the burden on farmers to the benefit of the merchants of the towns who controlled the legislature. He roused the whole of the west, and the governor declared a state of rebellion. On January 25, 1787, an attack was mounted on the Federal arsenal at Springfield. Shays's 1,200 men were repulsed, and scattered. But despite their defeat, they were pardoned under popular pressure.

On the frontier, meanwhile, feeling abandoned by the Congress in New York (where it had moved from Philadelphia), the settlers, surrounded as they were by trackless wilderness and potentially hostile Indians, looked elsewhere for protection. The settlers in what is now eastern Tennessee had already established a provisional government as the "State of Franklin," with revolutionary war hero *John Sevier* as provisional governor. Others in the newly opened areas of present day West Virginia, North Carolina, Georgia, and Alabama attached their small settlements to the new "state." Enraged by congressional neglect and realizing the need to open trade on the Mississippi if the new state was to survive, Sevier appealed for help to the Spanish ambassador, the Captain-General of Cuba, and the Governor of Louisiana. Writing to the first-named, he declared:

> The people of this region are aware which is the nation from whom their happiness and safety will depend in the future, and foresee that their interest and prosperity are thoroughly linked to the protection and liberality of your government.

Similarly, yet another revolutionary veteran settled in Kentucky, General James Wilkinson, also made moves toward Spain. The general fomented an independence movement in his area, based again upon abandonment by the national authorities and lack of protection against Indians. He wrote twice to King Charles III of Spain, swearing allegiance to him, asking for help and trading rights on the Mississippi. But as with Sevier's case, the King, although sympathetic to the plight of the western settlers (and not adverse to maintaining what he considered his rights in West Florida), was not interested in destroying the United States. He had in fact subsidized the building of St. Peter's church in New York City (where St. Elizabeth Anne Seton later converted) two

years earlier, and took a sympathetic view to the new nation—provided of course that it did not attempt to seize his
own dominions. We shall see how he was repaid later.

While it would be easy today to see Shays, Sevier, and
Wilkinson as traitors, it was not so apparent then. Had not
the government which they opposed itself been created in a
revolution—a revolution which all three had themselves fought
in? Did not Shays's farmers and Sevier's and Wilkinson's pioneers have the right to judge whether it had become necessary for them "to dissolve the political bands which have
connected them with another...," even as the Declaration of
Independence proclaimed?

Prior to the revolution, loyalty to the Crown was considered, as we have seen, to be both the bond of union between
the diverse peoples of the Empire and a religious duty; this
view was retained by the Loyalists. Their opponents, however, maintained (at least for public consumption) that self-
interest on the part of the people was the sole criterion in
government. But however effective this belief was in break-
ing down an established order, it was not a stable foundation
for a new one. It was in fact the same dilemma faced by the
Protestant leadership after their revolt against the Church.
Private judgment was the rallying cry which enabled people
to leave the Church—but how could one have any kind of
religious structure based on it? The answer in both cases would
be the same: continuing to pay lip-service to the ideal which
was used to justify the revolt, while rejecting it in practice.

# THE START OF THE
# FEDERAL GOVERNMENT

It was apparent by 1787 that the United States could not
long continue as they were. Sooner or later the states and the
pioneers would go each their separate ways, after which Great

Britain or Spain would absorb all or part of them. The leaders in each of the states decided that the Articles of Confederation must be revised. So, in 1787, the states sent delegates to Philadelphia in order to do so. George Washington was made chairman of the Constitutional Convention, and such notables as Franklin, Madison, and Alexander Hamilton were present. To avoid any criticism on the part of the public, the meetings were held in secret.

As they deliberated, the delegates' purpose changed. Rather than revising the Articles, they determined that what was needed was the creation of a Federal government with effective powers—in a word, of a government that would take the place of the Crown. Naturally, many of the states, particularly the smaller ones, feared that such a government would be dominated by the greater states and run for their profit. The larger ones pointed out that they would be expected to bear the brunt of the new government's expense. The compromise worked out was that of a two chamber Congress. The Senate would consist of two senators from each state, appointed by the state government; this body would serve as both the protector of the smaller states' interests, and of the states as a whole against the Federal government. The lower chamber, the House of Representatives, would consist of congressmen chosen on the basis of population; there the larger states would prevail. To become law, a bill would have to be passed by both houses. Thus a major block was broken.

But there were a few others. One was that, as the states were to be assessed their taxes and receive their number of representatives on the basis of population, some agreement had to be reached on the status of slaves. If they were not to be counted because of their unfree status, the slave states (which at this time included such northern states as New York and Pennsylvania, as well as the South) would pay much lower taxes. But if they were counted as part of the population, the slave states' representation in Congress would be much larger (even though the slaves would not vote). The compromise was typically American: five slaves would be counted as the equivalent of three free men. Further, the slave trade would become illegal in 1808 (a measure opposed as much by the New England shippers who brought the human cargo in as by those who bought it).

Another bone of contention was the commerce question. While it was obvious to the delegates that if the Congress were to function at all it must be able to regulate trade, the Southerners feared that the North, with its greater population, would for its own benefit strangle the trade necessary for Southern survival. The compromise attained here was that Congress was forbidden to tax exports, to favor one port over another, or to interfere with the slave trade until its 1808 abolition. Apart from these reservations, Congress would have the power "To regulate commerce with foreign nations, and among the several States, and with the Indian tribes." Interestingly enough, this last provision conferred a sort of status upon the Indian tribes analogous to that of foreign nations or the states. But the precise nature of that status has never been determined, and has been a source of difficulty ever since.

To prevent, as was said, tyranny, the government was divided into three sections: legislative, judicial, and executive. This last was to be the President. One conflict over this position was whether it should be directly elected or else appointed by Congress. It was pointed out that if Congress appointed him, the President would be dependent upon that body, and the independence of the post would be lost. On the other hand, Shays's Rebellion was fresh in the minds of the delegates. Moreover, many had been involved with whipping up popular anger against the King, and knew from personal experience how popular opinion could be manipulated. How to prevent others from doing what they themselves had done? The solution was found in the creation of an Electoral College, made of prominent local people who would themselves be popularly elected, and would in turn elect the President and Vice President (who would be the candidate with the second highest number of electoral votes). These would be, it was supposed, the same sort of substantial men who had brought about the revolution, continued to dominate many of the state governments, and had in fact been selected as delegates to the Convention itself.

The Supreme Court and inferior courts were envisaged as the third branch of government, which would have judicial power. To them would go disputes between states, and appellate power to decide on such cases brought them from lower courts as they were willing to hear. But note that the power of judicial review, through which abortion, for instance, has become the law of the land (through the Supreme Court determining that laws against it are somehow "unconstitutional") is nowhere to found in the constitution. It developed. It is precisely in this field of law, however, that an important factor in American history was implanted.

In Great Britain, where party strife between Whig and Tory, and between factions in those parties, was so acrimonious, the Monarchy served (and serves) as a stabilizing factor. Being in theory above mere party politics, it provides a focus of loyalty to authority available to those whose party is out of power—thus reducing the chance that they will take to violence to seize power. Indeed, the revolution against George III's personal government which was accomplished through bloodshed in this country was done through peaceful means in the mother country. An important part of this system are the law courts of the Crown, who are supposed to administer justice impartially and above all apolitically. Before them, a man stands not as a Whig or a Tory, but as a subject with rights thereby. This idea of an apolitical judiciary, so important for a stable society, was adopted along with the English common law by the states and then by the Federal government. From that time until our own day (when the courts have been increasingly politicized) it has provided much of the stability that a government otherwise dominated by party strife would normally lack; it has been an important factor in establishing the United States as a great power as a result.

There is another stabilizing factor which monarchy brings, and which the United States must somehow supply if they were to prosper. That is the sacredness of civil authority, seen as coming from God (which we described in the last chapter). The criticism of C.S. Lewis regarding opponents of monarchy is very apt:

> Monarchy can easily be debunked, but watch the faces, mark well the debunkers. These are the men whose taproot in Eden has been cut: whom no rumor of the polyphony, the dance, can reach—men to whom pebbles laid in a row are more beautiful than an arch. Yet even if they desire mere equality they cannot reach it. Where men are forbidden to honor a king they honor millionaires, athletes or film stars instead: even famous prostitutes or gangsters. For spiritual nature, like bodily nature, will be served; deny it food and it will gobble poison.

While the truth of Lewis's charges in America's cultural sphere is obvious, it is not quite so politically. Indeed, the political application of the principle in most countries has generally resulted in the elevation to power of men like Napoleon, Hitler, and Peron. This has not happened here. Why?

The answer may be found in the creation of a sort of secular religiosity, whose object of worship is the abstract will of the people, and which takes the place of much of the liturgy offered to God which surrounds Christian monarchy. In place of the crown jewels, we have the flag and icons like the Liberty Bell, and originals of the Declaration of Independence, the Constitution, and the Bill of Rights (of which more presently). These are all considered more or less sacred (all nations have flags, but few if any indulge in the sort of flag-worship we do–hedged about as it is with an elaborate ritual; obviously this fulfills a basic human need). The inauguration of the President has come to have all the pomp of a coronation. The Pilgrim and Founding Fathers are now saints whose opinions are tantamount to holy writ, and the 4th of July and Thanksgiving which honor them are the equivalents of Christmas and Easter for many. Obviously, this was not consciously planned; but it has had the result of supplying to these states the other great bulwark against anarchy and dictatorship. For the Catholic it does have one major drawback: it is a religion which is not Christian, and smacks of false worship. But it has been absolutely essential to the growth of a country whose unity has no real spiritual foundation, and has ensured that foreign strongmen have had here merely pale shadows like Andrew Jackson and Franklin Roosevelt. Its decline since the 1960's has been very dangerous to the well-being of the nation as it is presently constituted; from that point of view, President Reagan's call in his 1988 farewell address for a revival of civic ritual makes perfect sense.

Be that as it may, the development of this civic ritual was at once an eventual product of and an essential ingredient for the success of the Constitution composed in 1787. Without it, several flaws in the document would have ensured a great deal more civil strife than we have actually undergone. For while the Constitution did set up the framework of a government, it made no attempt to define the values under which that government would be administered. There was no mention of God, for example. So what system of morality would determine the conduct of public life? Religiously, the Founding Fathers were a varied bunch, the more important being Deists, and the remainder having varying degrees of attachment to the tenets of wildly diverging faiths. All alike had a certain adherence, however, to an aristocratic code of conduct, that code of honor which a Deist like Franklin and a Catholic like John Carroll could both agree on. But this code, based not upon an actual religion but upon a particular expression of European, specifically English, culture, could not long endure by itself. The American national religion arose to replace it, and for long provided the spiritual underpinnings without which the Constitution cannot operate successfully.

## The Emergence of Parties

Although the Constitution was adopted by the Convention delegates, it had to be ratified by at least nine of the states. Since the state legislatures would be extremely reluctant to give up their power to the proposed central government, the delegates recommended that the document be submitted to special popularly elected state conventions. The Constitution itself provided that if it was adopted by nine states, it would take effect in those states; practically, however, it had to be ratified by the four large states of Massachusetts, New York, Virginia, and Pennsylvania.

The opponents of the document were called *Anti-Federalists*. These were a loose coalition of debtors, farmers, and paper money supporters, who feared that the creation of a powerful Federal government would lead to ruin of state and local governmental independence, dominance by the wealthy, and eventual extinction of personal freedom. They were what would come to be known as populists. Patrick Henry, one of their foremost spokesmen, put their case with his usual eloquence:

Here is a revolution as radical as that which separated us from Great Britain. It is as radical if in this transition our rights and privileges are endangered, and the sovereignty of the States will be relinquished...

This Constitution is said to have beautiful features; but when I come to examine these features, sir, they appear to me to be horribly frightful. Among other deformities, it has an awful squinting. It squints toward monarchy; and does not this raise indignation in the breast of every true American?

The *Federalists* were the Constitution's supporters. They tended to comprise coastal populations, particularly merchants who were concerned with having a government capable of protecting their trade; those who lived more closely to the frontier or the borders and in regions fought over during the revolution, for military reasons. Particularly, those who believed most firmly in the United States as an instrument of world progress and redemption favored it. In any case, arguments such as Alexander Hamilton's summed up their position:

There is an idea, which is not without its advocates, that a vigorous executive is inconsistent with the genius of republican government....Energy in the executive is a leading character in the definition of a good government. It is essential to the protection of the community against foreign attacks; it is not less essential to the steady administration of the laws; to the protection of property against those irregular and high-handed combinations which sometimes interrupt the ordinary course of justice; to the security of liberty against the enterprises and assaults of ambition, of faction, and of anarchy....A feeble executive implies a feeble execution of the government. A feeble execution is but another phrase for a bad execution; and a government ill executed, whatever it may be in theory, must be, in practice, a bad government.

It was a compelling argument, well articulated in the series co-written by Hamilton and Madison, *The Federalist Papers*. Through the course of 1788, all the states except Rhode Island and North Carolina adopted it; reluctant states like New York being assured that, should the Constitution indeed bring about despotic government, the states would be able to secede. Without this understanding, several would not have ratified it. For the next 77 years, secession remained the ultimate threat whenever tension between various of the states and the Federal government grew extremely hot.

Within two years Rhode Island and North Carolina both acceded to the Union. But the opposition of the Anti-Federalists was not without effect, because it brought about the adoption of the first ten amendments to the Constitution, the Bill of Rights. These were intended to safeguard the personal freedoms of the people against possible despotism. Let us look at each in turn.

The first amendment declares that Congress "shall make no law respecting an establishment of religion, or of prohibiting the free exercise thereof..." While this is taken today to mean that there was to be a "wall of separation between Church and state," (leading to the conclusion that religious symbols may not be erected on public property, prayers and Christmas pageants may not be permitted in public schools, and so on), this is not so. Rather, since several of the states had their own established churches and others had none, Congress was not to have the right to establish one of their own; this was a question reserved to the states. Similarly, Congress could not proscribe any religion. The amendment went on to declare that Congress could not restrict freedom of speech or of the press, nor the right of the people to assemble or petition.

Next came the second amendment, which protected, in the interests of providing a well-armed militia, the right of private citizens to bear arms. Today, this amendment is at the center of the gun-control debate. Proponents of gun-control maintain that the existence of the National Guard as the State Militia satisfies this amendment; opponents declare that the right of individuals to own guns is essential to American freedom.

The third and fourth amendments required respectively that a) no troops could be quartered in private homes in peace time; and b) that such homes could not be entered by authorities without search warrants issued by a judge upon proof of just cause.

Trial by jury was required, and double-jeopardy cases forbidden, by the fifth amendment. The sixth ordered speedy trials, forbade trial of the accused outside the district where the alleged infraction occurred, and required that he be able to confront his accusers. He was also guaranteed, among others things, the right to defense counsel. Amendment VII guaranteed that trial by jury was preserved in major lawsuits, and the common law was given force here. The eighth forbade excessive bail or fines, as well as "cruel and unusual punishment." At the time of adoption, this latter was held to consist of torture, boiling in oil, drawing and quartering, and that sort of thing. Today it is often declared to be the death penalty itself.

The ninth amendment said that the rights given the people in the Constitution were not intended to deny others. The tenth is today the most forgotten: it restricts the powers of the federal government to those expressly given it in the Constitution.

The Federalists remained a party, considered more aristocratic and oriented toward Britain. They favored a loose construction of the Constitution. Hamilton and John Adams became some of their more prominent leaders. The Anti-Federalists became known eventually as members of what were called the Democratic-Republicans; apart from Patrick Henry, such supporters of the Constitution as its author Madison and Thomas Jefferson became its leaders. The Democratic-Republicans would favor a strict construction of the Constitution and friendly relations with France–the more so after the French Revolution. But while they were considered the equivalents of conservative and liberal at the time, and as we shall see their struggles would become extremely bitter, at base, they shared an ideology. There was a hollowness, an artificiality about their opposition to one another which has always characterized American politics.

Whence comes this strange unity, despite the often strident disagreements between parties? Apart from shared adherence to the secular American religion, it stems from three sources. First, the struggle is always over means rather than ends. No major political faction has ever seriously questioned the basic beliefs of the founding fathers, that the country exists solely to promote "life, liberty, and the pursuit of happiness," or in other words, economic growth. Profit for some, and at least subsistence for the majority; than this there is nothing higher, so that all questions of public morality are purely relative. There are never political principles but rather opinions, which the two major parties (whose names have changed over the course of history) exchange on a regular basis. When the two have a consensus on a given issue (such as that developing between Democrats and Republicans today on the merits of abortion) those who disagree simply do not exist politically.

Secondly, the extremely nebulous and ever-changing nature of the country's ruling class makes it adaptable to virtually any situation. While the folk who engineered the revolution were either landholding aristocrats or merchant patricians, their descendants did not necessarily remain part of the nation's ruling class. Stephen Birmingham in his *America's*

*Secret Aristocracy* (pp.9-10) treats of their withdrawal from public life:

> In the early days of the Republic, the American aristocracy simply assumed that its members would run the new country—as presidents, governors, senators, cabinet members, ambassadors—just as the British Aristocracy ran England. It was not until America's seventh president, the log-cabin-born Andrew Jackson, that a man entered the White House who was neither a member of the old Virginia landed gentry nor an Adams from Boston...
>
> In the years since Jackson, Americans continued to elect occasional members of the aristocracy to the presidency—up to and including Franklin D. Roosevelt—but the aristocracy itself had already become sorely disillusioned about the notion of American rulership and running for high political office....Gradually, it became merely prudent for the American aristocracy to turn to other less visible—and less vulnerable—forms of public service. Today, the American upper class shuns politics, and whether that is the country's gain or loss can only be a subject for speculation.

While, as we shall see, this retirement was not always as graceful as Mr. Birmingham suggests, it certainly did occur. In America, the upper class and the ruling class may contain a few of the same individuals, but they are emphatically not the same thing.

For entrance into the ruling class is solely dependent upon two things: money and adherence to the basic ideology of the existing membership. It is certainly not hereditary, nor is it based upon where the money comes from. At one time its leading professions were agriculture and trade, then banking and industry, and today they appear to be high finance and media. But the source of the funds is secondary to the thing itself. Obviously, however, such a diverse crowd is difficult to identify; moreover, there are an infinite number of degrees of "ins" and "outs," not unlike an onion. Where one belongs in the onion often changes back and forth during one's career.

The third factor in this underlying unity is the Masonic Order, which carries on today many of the functions of a state church. Most of our presidents have belonged to it, the White House, Capitol Building, and Washington Monument were all dedicated with its rites, and Washington himself swore the oath of office upon a Masonic bible (the same one, incidentally, used by George Bush). Apart from this overarching presence (and the pride which the Order takes in its part during the Revolution), it is an important force outside the centers of power, also. Across the country, wherever the small towns are not primarily Catholic (and in some which are) lack of membership in the local lodge is the equivalent of social and economic ostracism. Nor must it be overlooked that with the division of American Freemasonry into the York and Scottish rites, many different degrees and innumerable affiliated organizations, it is a difficult thing to characterize. Suffice it to say that it exists to safeguard the principals of Freemasonry, which have become the generally accepted principles of the United States. Except at its highest levels, American (and British, Canadian, and Australasian) Freemasonry has no need to adopt the nastily anti-Catholic attitudes and tactics employed by their brethren in Europe and Latin America. Here they are the establishment, and can afford to be apparently nice. Further, it must also be recognized that most of their membership here are not concerned or even aware of the Order's ultimate goals; just as it ought also be remembered that they frequently bicker with one another.

All of which having been said, both Anti-Federalists and Federalists united to throw all the electoral votes behind

George Washington, who became President in 1789, the same year as the beginning of the Revolution in Europe, which would topple our ally Louis XVI, and many another sovereign.

## THE FEDERALIST ERA

The first Congress elected under the new Constitution likewise met in 1789. Despite Washington's offer to serve without pay, they voted him a salary of $25,000 per year. Further, it was voted to form the Federal court system, and to set aside a ten square mile district to serve as the site of a capital to be built. Consisting of land donated on either side of the river Potomac by Maryland (which lost thereby Georgetown) and Virginia (similarly bereft of Alexandria), it was to be called the District of Columbia.

Soon after his inauguration at New York (shortly after which the capital returned to Philadelphia), Washington appointed a cabinet. In this, he departed from the British practice. With them, the cabinet was responsible not to the King but to whichever party was in control of Parliament. The Prime Minister was and is leader of that party, and responsible for selecting the other ministers and determining governmental policy. While the King or Queen continues to "appoint" the Prime Minister, it is done solely on the basis of parliamentary majorities, the monarch's preferences being immaterial.

But Washington set the precedent whereby the cabinet was chosen by himself (although Congress confirmed it), and acted as his own Prime Minister. Every President has done so, down to this day. But wanting to ensure that various opinions were represented, he appointed Jefferson as his Secretary of State, and Hamilton as his Secretary of the Treasury. The moderate federalist General Henry Knox became

Secretary of War.

Where Washington differed from more recent Presidents was in his reluctance to express views on legislation before it went before Congress, or to try to influence national opinion. In his view, the chief executive was not empowered to interfere in the business of Congress.

Hamilton's economic policy, which Washington supported, centered on the creation of a national bank which would hold public funds, and issue bank-notes to ensure a solid currency for the country. The power to create such a bank was nowhere to be found in the Constitution; but on this point Washington favored the Federalists and "loose" construction. It was not expressly forbidden, after all. So, despite Jefferson's bitter opposition, the Bank of the United States was chartered in 1791. The same year saw the admission of Vermont as the 14th state.

Another of Hamilton's economic measures approved by Congress were taxes on whisky, carriages, slaves, lands, and houses. There was no income tax, this being forbidden as confiscatory taxation in the Constitution. Additionally, tariffs were put on imports; not merely to raise money but to protect American made products against cheaper foreign products. A sign of growth on the frontier was the admission of the Commonwealth of Kentucky as the 15th state in 1792. Another sign of things to come in that momentous year was the invention of the cotton gin, which, by revolutionizing the growing of cotton, provided a stimulus for plantations devoted to the crop. The result was to make slavery, for long an unprofitable enterprise in slow decline, once again economically attractive. This in time would blow new life into "the peculiar institution."

# THE FRENCH REVOLUTION

Events in France, in the meantime, had risen to a fever pitch. In 1789, the Old Regime in France was ended, for the most part due to action by wealthy bourgeoisie and nobility—folk very similar to and with many of the same ideas as those who had brought about the American revolution. Such figures as La Fayette were prominent in both actions. Louis XVI was expected to continue to rule as a constitutional monarch, similar to George III since the fall of Lord North's government. But it was not to be. The revolution in France became ever more radical, and the King was deposed in 1792. He would be executed early the next year. Soon after, a slave revolt decimated the French colony of Saint Domingue (ending eventually, after much bloodshed and several invasions, with the establishment of the black republic of Haiti). The French Revolution had several direct results in the United States and adjoining areas.

In the West Indies, French refugees settled in the Spanish possessions of Santiago de Cuba and Trinidad, Gallicizing the Spanish spoken in the former and the culture of the latter. Large numbers of both Saint Dominguan planters and their slaves and Royalists from France arrived and set up plantations in New Orleans and St. Martinville, Louisiana. The second named became so sophisticated as a result that it was long called "Petit Paris," and many of its present day inhabitants pride themselves on their noble descent. Within the boundaries of the United States, the emigres arrived in all the major ports: Boston, New York (where the saintly black barber Toussaint arrived with a French family), Philadelphia, Wilmington (where settled the famed du Pont de Nemours clan), Baltimore, Charleston, and Savannah all received French emigres who at once refined manners in their places of refuge and either reinforced or introduced Catholicism there. Such towns as Gallipolis, Ohio were founded specifically as refuges for the French.

With these layfolk came also a flock of clerics, among whom were such names renowned in Catholic history as Bruté, Flaget, and Cheverus. To them do we owe the rapid extension of the Church into frontier territories–not merely to the French-speaking settlements in the old Northwest, but also to the extensive ones in Kentucky settled by Marylanders. Under their aegis, the anti-Roman spirit of Carroll was for a time diluted.

However unfortunate their uprooting was to themselves, the presence of these exiles in America was an unmixed blessing. But still the United States had to adopt some attitude toward the French Republic, which, having declared war against both altar and throne, was soon embroiled with Great Britain, Spain, Prussia, Austria, Russia, and various other lands, in a series of conflicts which would not end until 1815, at Waterloo.

The United States were allied to France by the 1778 treaty. Yet strong trade links with Britain had been re-established, and many of the Federalists deplored both the atheistic, anti-aristocratic, and anti-property aspects of the new regime. The dilemma was solved in 1793, when Washington, on his own authority, issued a proclamation of neutrality. This aroused great annoyance on the part of the Democratic-Republicans, who favored the ideals of the Jacobins, and who saw the European conflict as an excuse to seize Spanish territory. From this time, the two parties were in open opposition to one another, particularly as Jefferson resigned from the cabinet in protest at Washington's French policy. So the origin of our party system may in reality be set at the feet of the French Revolutionaries.

## Rebellion and Diplomacy

While the new federal taxes were accepted in most places with little complaint, they were bitterly resented in western Pennsylvania, where the manufacture of whisky in home stills was an important source of income to the Scotch-Irish farmers of the area, who often had no other profitable means of disposing of their grain. After a few years of building resentment, a group of these farmers armed themselves, threatened the revenue agents, and refused to pay the tax. Washington ordered federal troops dispatched to the area, and the rebellion was crushed. The new government had shown it could resist internal insurrection. Yet it was ironic that the government's troops were led by officers who a mere two decades before had themselves been rebels.

Nevertheless, relations with Great Britain were steadily improving. On November 19, 1794 John Jay signed in London a "Treaty of amity, commerce, and navigation" with the British. This provided for a settlement of certain financial claims the British had remaining against the United States, in return for which they at last evacuated the posts on American soil which they had occupied for so long.

The next year saw another treaty signed, this time with Spain. Under its provisions, Spain recognized the American claims in northern West Florida, and agreed to evacuate all posts in the formerly disputed territory (although Natchez, Mississippi, for example, remained in Spanish hands until 1798). Even more importantly, however, the right of free navigation on the Mississippi and deposit at the port of New Orleans was conceded to the Americans.

Washington's second term was crowned with admission in 1796 of Tennessee as the 16th state. But the "Father of His Country" was disgusted by and fearful of the increasingly nasty tone of debate between Federalists and Democratic-Republicans. In addition, he was getting older and his health was failing. He resolved to retire to Mount Vernon, and on September 18, 1797 delivered his farewell address. In this speech, he warned against both foreign entanglements and political factionalism–advice generally ignored by his successors. In the ensuing election, John Adams garnered the larger number of electoral votes and the presidency, with Jefferson coming up second, and so becoming vice president.

## The Adams Administration

John Adams had a very large set of shoes to fill, and a set of problems which daunted even his great predecessor. The Terror in France had made its mark on public, especially Federalist, opinion. Democratic Republicans were very vocal in their support of the French revolutionaries in their attempts to conquer all Europe, spearheaded by a newly famous General, Napoleon Bonaparte. Further, while many of the new immigrants came to this country to escape the revolutions in Europe, others came to foment strife here. How to deal with a threat which had sunk so many older and stronger countries in blood?

Adams had the Alien and Sedition laws passed through a Federalist dominated Congress as frightened of upheaval as he was. The Alien Act permitted the president to expel from the United States any foreigner he thought dangerous to the United States; the Sedition Act forbade any criticism of the President or Congress, and under its provisions a few newspaper editors were jailed. Although they provoked an hysterical reaction in many quarters and cost the Federalists a number of supporters, they were in fact the mildest national security measures ever adopted in the United States during a national emergency. It was a more innocent time.

Nevertheless, since the folk of those times could not foresee the future, many were enraged. The result were the Virginia and Kentucky Resolutions, co-authored by Jefferson and Madison. These declared that the Alien and Sedition Acts were void in the named states, being a violation of their sovereignty under the Constitution; these resolutions were in fact classic expositions of States' Rights theory.

Meanwhile, an undeclared naval war broke out with the French Revolutionaries on the high seas, adding to the general atmosphere of gloom, a gloom heightened by the death of Washington on December 14, 1799. There is a fairly well known story that Washington converted to the Faith on his deathbed, being received by Fr. Leonard Neale, S.J. Let us hope it is true.

The election of 1800 saw the defeat of Adams by Jefferson, and the filling of the Vice-Presidency by Aaron Burr, the runner-up. The election of Jefferson was felt by the most extreme Federalists to presage the fall of this country into the horrors of the French Revolution. But although these fears went unfulfilled, enough changes would result from it that the name "Revolution of 1800" is justified.

On November 22, 1800, Congress met for the first time at Washington, in a capitol as yet uncompleted. As one of his last acts, John Adams appointed *John Marshall* as Chief Justice of the Supreme Court. A Federalist loose constructionist, Marshall would continue to hand down decisions based upon his and Adams's shared philosophy of law for the next thirty-four years while the Federalist Party withered, died, and at last vanished from memory. But as we shall see, he made the Supreme Court what it was until the middle of this century, and served longer than any other Chief Justice.

## The Failure of the Federalists

Although no one knew it at the time, the inauguration of Jefferson on March 4, 1801 spelled the end of the Federalists. They would continue on as an ever diminishing minority for the next fifteen years, but they would not be an effective force again (although their ghost would continue on the Supreme Court). It will be instructive to look at the reasons for their failure.

On the surface, part of their problem was simply in being the party of strong government. It was one thing to boast that they were the men of experience, an aristocracy, in the sense of a ruling class by virtue of being better at ruling. But what if the Democratic-Republicans in office should in the end prove as or more successful than they were themselves?

From a Catholic point of view, it is rather a complex thing to try to determine which of the two was the party most in accord with the Church's teaching; both had good elements and ideas; both had bad ones; both were dedicated to a system basically in conflict with the social doctrines of the Church.

*Subsidiarity* is one of the most basic of these last. It is the belief that in governance, acts are best carried out by the smallest unit capable of doing so. In Catholic Europe, this meant that, in ascending order, the parishes (in a civil sense), the bailiwicks, and the provinces of the different kingdoms, with their parallel religious hierarchies of abbots, bishops and archbishops, and noble ones of barons, counts, dukes, and so forth, all administered affairs to the height of their capacity. To the King was reserved the ultimate appeal in justice, war and foreign affairs, roads and posts, and certain forests and waters. Centralizing tendencies on the part of various Kings played a large part in the Protestant Revolt, and the French Revolutionaries perfected it in the "One and Indivisible Republic." So it was that the opposition to them, as in Tyrol and the Vendee, demanded their local liberties back, along with their Church and King. The same was true in the 19th and early 20th centuries of the Legitimists in

France, the Carlists in Spain, the Miguelists in Portugal, and of course the opponents of Bismarck and Cavour in the German and Italian states.

In American terms, the closest that we may come to subsidiarity under the religious, economic, social, and political conditions which have prevailed from 1783 to the present is States' Rights. So in this aspect, the Democratic-Republicans, when they remained true to their stated platform (which as we will see did not always happen—for good as for ill—when they were in power) were correct, and the Federalists were wrong.

But as regards their views on the French Revolution, we must change sides. For the Federalists believed it to be evil, and Democratic-Republicans supported it. So great was the horror of the Federalists at the atrocities in France, that it even caused some of them to re-examine their attitudes toward the Catholic Faith. In a sermon of July 4, 1798, the rigid Calvinist minister and president of Yale, Timothy Dwight, among many charges against the Jacobins listed:

> 2. The overthrow of the religious orders in Catholic countries, a step essentially necessary to the destruction of the religion professed in those countries.

While the truth of the statement had always been maintained by his co-religionists, its denunciation as a crime if put into practice would have been unthinkable a decade or two before, when all New England would have considered it "a consummation devoutly to be wished."

But the realities of revolution led by others (as opposed to that led by themselves) forced many to think more sensibly on political topics then they had while engaged in rebellion against King George. *Fisher Ames*, for example, one of the most brilliant Federalists, wrote in 1805:

> The people, as a body, cannot deliberate. Neverthe-

less, they will feel an irresistible impulse to act, and their
resolutions will be dictated to them by their demagogues.
The consciousness, or the opinion, that they possess the
supreme power will inspire inordinate passions; and the
violent men, who are the most forward to gratify those
passions, will be their favorites. What is called the government of the people is in fact too often the arbitrary
power of such men.

This is in fact an analysis which, while perhaps strange
to Catholics of today, is perfectly in keeping with the Church's
traditional teaching on the point. Compare these words of
Pius VI in his allocution of July 17, 1793, *Pourquoi Nôtre
Voix*:

> The most Christian King, Louis XVI, was condemned
> to death by an impious conspiracy and this judgment
> was carried out. We shall recall to you in a few words the
> ordering and motives of this sentence. The National
> Convention had no right or authority to pronounce it.
> In fact, after having abolished the monarchy, *the best of
> all governments*, it had transferred all the public power to
> the people–the people which, guided neither by reason
> nor by counsels, forms just ideas on no point whatso-
> ever, assesses few things in accordance with the truth and
> evaluates a great many according to mere opinion, which
> is ever fickle, and ever easy to deceive and to lead into
> every excess, ungrateful, arrogant, and cruel...(cap. 2).

Very similar, indeed. The Pope's words, and others like
them, brought forth reactions from Catholics of all classes
throughout France and the rest of Europe. When his peas-
ant tenants came to his chateau in 1793, d'Elbée, soon to be
renowned as a key leader of the Vendee revolt, told them:

> My children, you know I have never deceived you;
> and I shall not deceive you now in this most important
> matter. The revolution is a fact: it will not, it cannot be

undone. It will devour all that is good in France; and our efforts can be but feeble against a power which strengthens every day. I am ready to die for God and my King; but I will not command men who are not worthy of being martyrs. Go back for this night to your cottages; reflect that an act of yours may set them on fire, and ruin your families; and weigh well what I have said to you. Tomorrow morning come back again, if God inspires you with courage to die; and then I will go with you.

Thus spoke a Catholic aristocrat; an eminent realist, who nevertheless shared the sentiments of Pius VI, and presumably, Fisher Ames. But what did the eminent Mr. Ames think was the proper course of action, given the principles he held? Replying to the attack by his logic-minded Democratic-Republican opponents that ideological Federalists must be Monarchists, he wrote in the essay earlier quoted:

It will weigh nothing in the argument with some persons, but with men of sense it will be conclusive, that the mass of the Federalists are the owners of the commercial and moneyed wealth of the nation. Is it conceivable that such men will plot a revolution in favor of monarchy, a revolution that would make them beggars as well as traitors if it should miscarry; and if it should succeed ever so well, would require a century to take root and acquire stability enough to ensure justice and protect property?

Here then, was the difference between Catholic counter-revolutionary and Protestant conservative; the one saw the battle with the Revolution as a fight of good against evil, truth against falsehood, and so a struggle worth any price; the latter saw in it merely a conflict between prudence and good sense on the one hand, and anarchy and demagoguery on the other. For this last-named, surely submission was wiser than resistance to the last? This has been the recipe for English speaking conservatives in the British Isles since the

Jacobite cause went down to defeat at Culloden, and on these shores either since the last Tory went to Canada or Lee surrendered at Appomattox. One may die for a principle, but never for an opinion. The Federalists, alas, had only opinions.

There is a reason for this, however. It is a maxim that all political questions are in essence religious. Although the Federalists often invoked the language of Christianity to bolster their arguments against the supposedly "Godless" Democratic-Republicans, their leadership often had precisely the same opinions as their opponents. This we have seen with John Adams and Jefferson. But this was true of many lesser ranking Federalist potentates as well. A typical case was Theodore Sedgwick, the biggest man in Berkshire County, Massachusetts. As recounted by David Hackett Fischer:

> The means by which Sedgwick controlled his county ought not to be confused with the methods of a modern party machine. The principal prop beneath his power was the habit of deference in the people. It was slipping, as Shays's Rebellion showed, but not yet down. Every act of Sedgwick's was designed to buttress it. Firstly, he sought to strengthen "the influence of numerous connexions formed into a phalanx by family compact," as Jefferson described it. Sedgwicks, Dwights, Van Schaights, Worthingtons, Masons, and Sergeants were intertwined in one extended cousinage, one "union of political influence" which allowed of no alternative to "rule by the wise and the good."
>
> Secondly, Sedgwick endeavored to promote "good order" in Berkshire County by means of an alliance with the established Congregational Church. Though he personally found Unitarianism attractive, his heresy remained a closely guarded secret until he made a deathbed confession to William Ellery Channing (*The Revolution of American Conservatism*, pp. 13-14).

There is the problem in a nutshell. Of what did Sedgwick's Conservatism consist? Loyalty to his sect? No, this was a mere hypocritical ploy to maintain "good order," whatever that might be. Loyalty to his King? Although he was, in Mr. Fischer's words, "a most reluctant rebel," "Doubts and mental reservations notwithstanding, Sedgwick committed himself unequivocally to the Whig cause." Yet how can an aristocrat who is loyal neither to his God nor his King call himself wise or good? It is a conundrum, but one may be sure that Sedgwick himself felt very idealistic indeed, while pursuing naked self interest—in which he shows he was a typical human being.

But the point here is that to succeed, a political party or faction requires a spirit of self-sacrifice. That is something which the Federalists, in common with many American "conservatives" since, lacked entirely. The more idealistic of them continued to enjoy their positions in local society, all the while denouncing their opponents futilely; the more pragmatic became Democratic-Republicans in order to "change the party from within." Whatever the case, the result was the same. The Federalists lost out to the Democratic-Republicans for one major reason. No matter how hotly they denounced them, or how much hatred they felt for them, they were in all that mattered identical to them—simply not as good at it as the Democratic-Republicans were. In the final analysis, that has been the story of the two parties ever since.

# THE REVOLUTION OF 1800

When Thomas Jefferson took the oath of office on March 4, 1801, radicals rejoiced and conservatives darkly prophesied. Both were doomed to disappointment. For Jefferson although an opponent of the powers the Federalists had acquired for the government when they were in control, was only too glad to retain and even extend them when he was President himself. He supported the use of Federal money for the building of roads and canals to bind the regions of the country more tightly together, a policy which, continued by his successors, led to the rapid settlement of the West.

An example of this may be found in Ohio. The present state of Ohio had become a sort of refuge for many tribes (like the Delaware) driven from the East. Together with Indians already resident, such as the Shawnee, they were a powerful impediment in the way of western settlement. War broke out between them and the ever encroaching settlers in 1790, and in the following two years they inflicted two crushing defeats on the American army. But in 1794, they were in turn defeated by the energetic veteran, "Mad" Anthony Wayne, at the battle of Fallen Timbers. The next year, the associated tribes signed an agreement with the United States, ceding most of southern and central Ohio to the government. Settlers from New England and the Pennsylvania Dutch country poured in via the opening trails, and by 1802, Ohio had a large enough population to be admitted as the 17th state. Western expansion was a large part of Mr. Jefferson's program.

Of course, he did make certain cosmetic bows to his principles. The court etiquette of the Federalist regime in the President's Palace was done away with. The Alien and Sedition Acts were repealed, as was the internal revenue measure that so annoyed the whisky producers. Jefferson never let an opportunity go by without praising the "common man."

Above all, his antagonism to the Federalists was most obvious in his dealing with the judiciary. Just prior to leaving office, Adams had appointed many "midnight judges." Jefferson instructed Madison, his Secretary of State, not to grant the commissions of several of these. One of them,

William Marbury, asked the Supreme Court for a court order which would force the government to render the commission. Finding for Marbury in 1803, Chief Justice Marshall established the doctrine of judicial review, under which the Supreme Court has decided whether or not laws brought before it are valid or "constitutional." Marshall declared that:

> The constitution is either a superior paramount law, unchangeable by ordinary means, or it is on a level with ordinary acts, and, like other acts, is alterable when the legislature shall please to alter it.

> If the former part of the alternative be true, then a legislative act contrary to the constitution is not law...

> It is emphatically the province and duty of the judicial department to say what the law is. Those who apply the rule to particular cases must of necessity expound and interpret that rule. If two laws conflict with each other, the courts must decide on the interpretation of each.

From that day to this, the Supreme Court has made judicial review its greatest privilege; indeed, it is now what most Americans think of as its primary function. But it is important to remember that while today (as in the case of abortion) Supreme Court decisions are held not merely to determine constitutionality but also intrinsic morality, it was not always so. There is nothing in the Constitution to warrant it.

## The Louisiana Purchase

However unconstitutional Jefferson may have thought Marshall's decision, he was able to equal it in his action in buying the French colony of Louisiana that same year.

Spain had been defeated by France under Bonaparte. As part of the treaty of San Idelfonso in 1800, Spain agreed to give Louisiana back to France. As Bonaparte was engaged in trying to reconquer Saint Domingue at the time, he planned to use Louisiana as a source of food for the highly profitable sugar colony Saint Domingue would become once again, after he subdued its rebellious blacks. But two years of fighting had failed to do so, and when he went to war with Britain once again in 1802, the military and naval supplies and troops (to say nothing of free use of the sea lanes to transport them) essential to eventual reconquest of the island had to be employed elsewhere. He would never be able to use Louisiana. Worse, the British might feel compelled to seize it themselves, and Napoleon had no real means of defending it.

Meanwhile, Jefferson was very intent on gaining control of the city of New Orleans and the Floridas (which remained Spanish; Louisiana also had not been officially transferred to France). He opened negotiations with Napoleon on the topic of acquiring New Orleans and whatever claims France might have in West Florida. Needless to say, this was not provided for in the Constitution. Nevertheless, Jefferson felt it imperative for the country's long range development. Moreover, American frontiersmen were moving into Louisiana; swearing allegiance to the Spanish Crown, of course, but taking their oaths as lightly as did their fathers their oaths to the British Crown at the time of the revolution. Jefferson was astounded when, instead of just New Orleans, Napoleon offered the whole of Louisiana for $15,000,000. The President bought, and on December 20, 1803, the Stars and Stripes were hoisted in New Orleans' *place d'armes*. Creoles wept, and the French commissioner, Laussat, burst into tears, saying "What a magnificent New France we have lost."

Indeed they had. But just what had Jefferson bought? The boundaries of Louisiana were very unsure; except for the island of Orleans upon which the city itself sits, the boundary of the territory to the east was the Mississippi. On the north and west, it was supposed to include all the lands drained by the great river and its tributaries. But as much of this was unexplored, no one really knew quite where Louisiana's frontiers really were. More than this, Jefferson claimed that the purchase entitled the US not only to this large territory, but to West Florida, Texas, and the Oregon country, thus bringing the country into land disputes not merely with Spain but with Great Britain and Russia also. But wherever the truth might lie, the area that was indisputably American doubled the size of the country at one stroke. Within this vast area were forests and prairies, rivers and the Rockies.

Settlement in this realm was quite varied. New Orleans itself was the equal of any European city in terms of sophistication; the city's Creole and emigre inhabitants had perfected the art of living to a degree unequaled anywhere on the continent outside the walls of Quebec. The public worship of the Church, balls, fine wines and food, music, literature, indeed, all that makes life pleasant were found there in a degree unknown to the United States, save perhaps in those ports where the French emigres had already begun their work. It is also true that the city suffered from recurrent bouts of yellow fever, filthy streets and various other ills; but the city's flaws were as much common property to cities of that day as its virtues were its own. Then as now, the graceful Spanish architecture of what was then the whole of the city and is now the Vieux Carré was unequaled.

Apart from the town of St. Martinville, the bayous and prairies nearest New Orleans were the domain of Acadian refugees. Much simpler than their Creole neighbors, they were strongly attached to their religion and way of life. Subsisting in isolation, their gentle demeanor and friendly acceptance of outsiders led them, until the pressures of assimilation after World War I began to take their toll, to absorb the outsiders who came their way. So today such un-French names as Schnexnayder and Abshire are considered as "Cajun" as Broussard and Hebert.

Up the river, in places like Arkansas Post and the Missouri towns of Ste. Genevieve, St. Louis, and St. Charles, attempts were made by the Creoles there to live with some of the *joie de vivre* their cousins maintained in New Orleans. There too, and everywhere the rivers extended in Louisiana, Creoles were joined by French Canadian trappers and traders, who carried both the French language and the Catholic Faith ever further into the interior. By this means, several tribes received a preparation for the Gospel which later missionaries like Fr. De Smet would benefit from.

What would have happened if the Louisiana territory had remained in French or Spanish hands? We cannot know. But surely the easy manner of living and intense piety which even today can be found in the southern parishes of Louisiana would extend throughout the center of nation; instead of being repeatedly moved and massacred, the Indians of those region might well have become, as Fr. De Smet wished, the inhabitants of something like the mission state of Paraguay.

In any case, Jefferson and his associates had little but contempt for the Creoles (as the President's hatred for their religion would make obvious). Although the treaty of cession obliged the Americans to give the inhabitants of Louisiana the same rights as their new fellow-citizens, Jefferson opined that they were "as yet as incapable of self-government as children." As a result, in March of 1804, when the purchase was divided in two (along the present Louisiana-Arkansas boundary), the southern Territory of Orleans, although specifically indicated as a possible future state, was denied any sort of self-government. The northern District of Louisiana, being primarily Indian territory, was not to become a state. So a people of immense culture were deprived of any political voice, while the hordes of illiterate frontiersmen who soon poured in, had the rights of citizens. Apparently Jefferson had forgotten the words he had written so long before in the Declaration, about the "just consent of the governed."

Immediately, Jefferson began fomenting trouble for the Spanish in West Florida, inciting various of their Anglo-American subjects to rebel, so as to be able to send in American troops to "restore order." Luckily, the Spanish had been able to suppress these without too much difficulty. But Spain also retained the post of Los Adaes east of the Sabine river in present day Louisiana, where lived a number of Spanish settlers and their Apache and Choctaw Indian allies. In 1806, Jefferson resolved to expel them. His Governor, William Claiborne, was all too aware that if war broke out between the Spanish and the Americans the disenfranchised Creoles would side with the Spanish. But he was able to outbluff the Spanish commander, and their troops withdrew into Texas.

## Diplomacy Elsewhere

Meanwhile, events overseas also took a great deal of Jefferson's attention. For several centuries the Barbary pirates of North Africa had taken slaves during raids on remote parts of Ireland and Iceland, and had bedeviled the shipping of European nations. Usually they were bought off from time to time with tribute. But the Americans refused to pay, and so found themselves involved in difficulties with the Pasha of Tripoli in 1804. In reprisal, Jefferson dispatched a force of seven marines under a Captain O'Bannon to assist a pretender to the throne in unseating the Pasha. The result of the war was a treaty with Tripoli in 1805, and the presentation of a scimitar to O'Bannon. Since then, US Marine officers have carried similar weapons, called today "Mameluke swords."

At the same time, Britain and France from time to time

in the course of their fighting one another would molest American ships and occasionally impress American sailors into their service. Things rose to a head after Jefferson's re-election in 1805. In 1806, the British forbade any ships to enter ports held by Napoleon; he in turn forbade any trading with Great Britain. American merchants thus fell between two stools. An attack by the British on an American ship in 1807 led to a total embargo on all trade with foreign nations; this act was passed by Congress on December 22, 1807.

The Embargo continued in full force until March 15, 1809, when it was repealed except with regard to France and Britain themselves. In that time, the American economy foundered. From Portland to New Orleans, ships and cargoes rotted at the docks. But the Embargo did have the result of reviving for a time the Federalists, who at last had an issue. But the promise of James Madison to loosen the Embargo were he elected took even that from them. Thus, on March 4, 1809, James Madison was duly sworn in, and except as regarded the prime perpetrators, the Embargo duly ended 11 days later.

## President Madison–Empire Builder

There were two major concerns facing Madison: foreign trade and national expansion. The first primarily revolved around the activities of the French and British warships. In 1810, the French swore off poaching American ships, and the Embargo was lifted as regarded them. But it was reaffirmed for Great Britain on February 2, 1811.

While all of this was underway, events in Spain were going from bad to worse. Napoleon on March 17, 1808 compelled both Charles IV and his son Ferdinand VII to abdicate the throne of Spain, whereupon he placed his brother Joseph on the throne. A revolt broke out almost immediately, and a parliament gathered in Seville which declared itself loyal to Ferdinand VII. In Spain's Empire, local officials were forced to choose between the two sides, shipments of arms and money from the motherland were cut off, and rebellions for or against Ferdinand broke out. In 1810, for example, the priest Hidalgo in Mexico led a bloody rising against the Spanish. While eventually suppressed, it had the effect (due to the blockade the rebels imposed on the Mexican port of San Blas) of isolating California from the rest of the Spanish world for eleven years. The Spanish officials and garrisons carried on, supported by the missionaries and rancheros there.

In the Floridas, so close to a United States which coveted them, and filled as they were becoming with American settlers, the situation was very dangerous. At last, on August 13, 1810, a convention of American settlers in Baton Rouge declared itself in charge of the district. They were in touch with Madison through the governor of the Mississippi Territory. On September 24, the conspirators seized the fort in Baton Rouge, captured the Governor, and three days later sent to Washington a "declaration of independence" detaching themselves from Spain and asking to be annexed to the United States. On October 27, Madison directed Claiborne to take control of Baton Rouge. From that time on, the area has been known as the "Florida Parishes" of Louisiana. This method having worked so well, Madison, leaving the Spanish in Mobile and Pensacola unmolested for the moment, turned his attention to East Florida and its capital of St. Augustine.

After Spain took control of East Florida from the British, the area between its northern boundary—the St. Mary's River—and St. Augustine began to fill up with settlers of various nationalities, all of whom took the oath to His Most Catholic Majesty (as indeed did the West Florida settlers).

The northernmost port of Florida, Fernadina, had become very wealthy in assisting Americans to evade the embargo. There Madison's stroke fell.

In March of 1811, a group of American irregulars took Fernadina, overpowering its nine-man garrison. Declaring the Republic of East Florida, they set off to conquer St. Augustine. The Americans first took Moosa, the site of a settlement of Catholic free blacks which had been destroyed by Oglethorpe in 1740. Proceeding to the walls of St. Augustine, they demanded that the Spanish surrender. The latter refused, and so the besiegers settled down. For over a year this situation continued. But as relations with Britain grew rockier (and Canada appeared more tempting), Madison decided to disavow the East Florida situation–particularly after Spanish reinforcements broke the siege in June of 1812.

After the War of 1812 broke out, the Spanish armed the Creek and Seminole Indians, and the many blacks who had fled slavery to go to Florida. Although the Americans duly occupied Mobile and Biloxi in 1812, reducing Florida to its present boundaries, and though the East Florida conflict eventually merged into the War of 1812, the rebels were finally cleared out. Florida would remain Spanish for a few more years.

## War with Britain

While Madison was busy with grabbing what Spanish territory he could, yet another Indian organizer in the tradition of King Philip and Pontiac had arisen. He was the Shawnee chief, Tecumseh. Organizing a confederation of Western tribes that stretched from the Canadian to the Spanish borders, he had also the support of the British. While in 1811 the governor of Indiana Territory, William Henry Harrison, defeated him at the battle of Tippecanoe, he merely withdrew into Canada and bided his time.

At the same time, the clamor in Congress for war with Britain among the *Warhawks,* a group of young congressmen led by *Henry Clay* and *John C. Calhoun,* grew ever more strident. They were not concerned with the continuing impressment problem, but thought it would serve as a good pretext to seize Canada.

At that time, Canada was made up largely of two very different groups: the French Canadians and the Loyalists who had been expelled from the United States. As these two groups were quite different from one another, and generally did not get along well, the two provinces of Ontario (shorn off Quebec) and New Brunswick (taken from Nova Scotia) were created to accommodate the English speakers. The supposed disunity of the two groups would, so the warhawks thought, make the invasion of Canada easy.

They were wrong. After war was declared on April 4, 1812, an invasion of Canada was mounted. It ended sooner than it began. The British with Tecumseh seized Detroit, and the American troops refused to leave Ft. Niagara. The next year the US won control of Lake Erie, but lost the Niagara forts. Nevertheless, control of the lake allowed the Americans to burn the Canadian capital of York (now Toronto). An attempt to take Montreal was foiled at Chateauguay by the gallant Colonel de Salaberry and a handful of French-Canadian militia. The British blockaded the Atlantic ports. On the other hand, Tecumseh was killed at the Battle of the Thames. This noble character, who had early distinguished himself by risking his life to prevent the slaughter of captives by Indian custom, was an enormous loss both to the British and to the Indians. But his allies the Creeks carried war to the Americans in the South, only to come up against one of the most remarkable figures America has produced: General *Andrew Jackson.* After defeating the hostile Creeks, he stripped both them and those who had fought for the United States of an enormous amount of acreage in Alabama. In this, of course, he was following the example of his commander in chief; after all—had not Spain been our ally too?

But 1814 also saw a great disaster befall American arms. A British fleet sailed up the Chesapeake. One column sailed off to attack Baltimore, the other Washington. Baltimore was preserved through the refusal of Ft. McHenry to surrender (an event witnessed, as everyone knows, by Francis Scott Key. So inspired by the event was he that he wrote the *Star Spangled Banner* to commemorate it. The tune he used was that jolly old drinking song *To Anacreon in Heaven*. Where the national anthem has, "O say does that star-spangled banner yet wave, o'er the land of the free and the home of the brave," the original says, "And so I will teach you like me to entwine, the myrtle of Venus with Bacchus' vine"). Washington did not fare so well. Four thousand American troops met the British at Bladensburg; all ran save 400 Marines, who were overwhelmed. When the British burned Washington in reprisal for the burning of York the previous year (one good capital deserves another, so to speak), they left untouched the house of the Commandant of the Marine Corps as a tribute to Marine valor at Bladensburg. In any case, Dolly Madison fled the President's Palace with a portrait of Washington (when she returned to the burnt-out shell, she had the building white-washed, hence the present name of White House).

All this time, New England had been left to shift for itself. Between the Embargo and the War, the region's economy had been ruined. To save themselves, the New England states sent representatives to Hartford, Connecticut to discuss secession from the Union. As Madison was driven by these calamities to seek peace, so too were the British, exhausted by years of struggle against Napoleon. A peace treaty was signed at Ghent on December 24, 1814, leaving all issues of contention basically undecided.

Unhappily, the news did not reach the New World in time to prevent the Battle of New Orleans, which raged around New Year's of 1815. General Jackson was able to repel an attempted British invasion—which, had it succeeded would have meant nothing as the treaty obligated Britain to withdraw from all US territory. But nevertheless, the victory of Jackson, with his scratch force of militia, regulars, Creoles, and Laffitte's pirates, was nothing short of miraculous. The people of the Crescent City have always regarded the victory as being due to the intercession of Our Lady of Prompt Succor.

By 1815, the United States were indeed a nation with an identity of their own. Much of the credit for this must go to Jefferson and Madison. But in the end, how must we evaluate them? Joseph Burkholder Smith gives a fair estimate in his account of the Florida plotting:

> Thomas Jefferson and his two disciples, James Madison and James Monroe, were promoted to the pantheon of the Founding Fathers, the American nationalist religion's temple, while all of them still lived. To bolster this status, sculptors of the time portrayed them in the costumes of ancient Rome....As for telling the truth to the American people, all three were Olympian when writing political philosophy. When running the government, their regard for the niceties of frank communication was Nixonian.

# ADOLESCENT AMERICA 1816-1848

## THE NATION IN 1816

The end of the War of 1812 found these United States greatly divided. New England merchants had received two great financial blows. The first was the abolition of the slave trade in 1808. As the human cargo was generally transported to America in New England ships, the loss of such profitable commerce was considerable, although some continued it secretly. On the other hand, the way was paved for New Englanders to eventually feel moral superiority to the South.

The second was the British blockade during the War of 1812. Cut off from British and other textiles, many New England merchants were forced to open cloth factories of their own, which continued after the war. Within ten years after the peace, the region was well on its way to becoming a great industrial center. This was to have several important effects.

The mass migration of Yankee farmers to the Ohio country commencing after the Revolution depopulated New

England's countryside; just at the time when a large cheap labor force was needed, it vanished. The result was that factory owners had to look overseas and to French Canada for workers. Their migration would, within a century, completely transform the area from a Puritan stronghold to a numerically Catholic one (although the Puritan imprint on local culture would never be uprooted; the immigrants would conform to it instead).

A particularly fateful effect was that this change from trade to manufacturing would put New England into direct conflict with the South. Before, Yankee politicians had opposed any tariffs which would restrict the free flow of profits to and from Boston, Salem, and the area's other ports. Despite the development of whaling and the China trade, when the economy shifted, regional politicians came to support high tariffs as a way to protect their products from foreign competition. Such profits for Boston, however, could only mean losses for the South, forced to rely on more expensive New England manufactured goods essential to the Southern plantation economy (which could not make such things for itself). Beyond this, the beginnings of New England's industrialization marks a development which would lead not only to Northern dominance over the South but in time would propel the United States to the position of most powerful nation in the world.

The South, in the meantime, continued to develop its unique culture. Unlike New England, the Southern states were geographically able to expand their way of life directly into the western frontier. As a result, Southern politicians tended to favor territorial expansion toward the Pacific. For the continuance of their economy, they required a flow of cheap manufactured goods; low tariffs would ensure this. The Southerners were therefore more than a little suspicious of Federal power.

The Middle States, sitting between the first two areas and blessed with the harbors of New York City and Philadelphia, had the potential for real wealth. This area serving also as natural outlets for the West's trade, their politicians were anxious for national roads and canals which would make such travel easier. Already, their merchants had acquired a great deal of local power. But in 1816, New York and Pennsylvania were still slave states, and very much dominated by the agricultural oligarchies which had run them since settlement.

The West was being settled fast. Mississippi was admitted in 1817, Illinois the next year, and Alabama the year after that. Pioneers both from Europe and the East filled up land as quickly as the Indians could be moved off of it. As might be expected, the latter were none too pleased at the prospect.

The election of 1816 brought in James Monroe and sealed the end of the Federalist Party; for the next eight years all the major figures in American politics would belong to the Democratic Republicans. This period would go down in history as *The Era of Good Feeling*.

Where Spain had been a real opponent prior to the French Revolution, her American possessions had been severely shaken by local revolts and occupation of the homeland by the French. Florida had been repeatedly invaded and portions shorn off by American forces. Some American settlers were already arriving in Texas, and dreams were even now being dreamed of its annexation by the United States. Under the Americanist Archbishop of Baltimore, John Carroll, America's few Catholics were not too concerned about their Spanish co-religionists.

## The States and Europe

The defeat of Napoleon at Waterloo in 1815 meant the

restoration of the various dynasties in Europe to their thrones. Centering on the friendship of the Emperors of Austria and Russia, and the King of Prussia, *the Holy Alliance* eventually was joined by all the rulers on the continent save three: the Pope, because he could not ally with non-Catholics; the Prince-Regent of Great Britain (who nevertheless declared his agreement with the Alliance's principles); and the Sultan of Turkey, who would not join with Christians. Despite being initially suggested by the Tsar of Russia, the Alliance ultimately owed its origin to the writings of Catholic German lay theologian *Franz von Baader*.

The treaty which established it may be found in Appendix II. From the Catholic point of view, there were a number of problems with the document. There was no mention of the Church of Christ; presumably Catholicism, heresy, and schism were all to have equal standing. The leading diplomats of the day, *Metternich, Castlereagh*, and others, all proclaimed it to be "sublime mysticism and nonsense."

Still, when all that can be said against the Alliance be said, there remains much in its favor. Whatever they may have thought privately, all Europe's sovereigns felt it necessary to sign. Such religious language had not been seen in a treaty since before the Protestant Revolt split Christendom—and the treaty's second article anticipated by over a century Pius XI's words in regard to the social Kingship of Christ in his 1925 encyclical, *Quas Primas*.

Moreover, the Alliance signaled a desire for a return to the *Res Publica Christiana*, a Europe which was really one Christendom—united temporally as well as spiritually. It was supported not only by von Baader, but by all the best Catholic political writers of the era—*Joseph de Maistre, Chateaubriand, Louis de Bonald, Adam Müller, Karl von Haller*, and many more. Most significant of all were those who opposed the Alliance in Europe; it was universally hated by all who hated the Church. Secret societies took oaths against it, liberal politicians derided its principles.

Where stood these United States? In common with their ideological allies in Europe, most politicians and newspapermen in America condemned the Alliance as both Catholic and monarchical–a tool of tyranny. Moreover, the adherence of Spain to the Alliance appeared to mean that Spanish America would henceforth be not quite so easy to annex. Indeed, might not a revived Spain, assisted by the rest of Europe, attempt to regain her lost territories in Louisiana and West Florida? John Quincy Adams commented in 1817 on the revolts against the Spanish:

> The republican spirit of our country not only sympathizes with people struggling in a cause so nearly if not precisely the same which was once our own, but it is working into indignation against the relapse of Europe into the opposite principle of monkery and despotism (*Writings of John Quincy Adams*, vol. VI, p.274).

Speaker of the House Henry Clay urged in May 1821:

> ...that a sort of counterpoise to the Holy Alliance should be formed in the two Americas...to operate by the force of example and by moral influence, that here a rallying point and an asylum should exist for freemen and for freedom (*Papers of Henry Clay*, vol. III, p.80).

It ought to be noted that both Clay and Adams were considered Conservatives in American terms.

## Florida, Mexico, and the End of Spanish America

Whatever fears the Holy Alliance might raise in American hearts, the reality was that the Spanish edifice in the new world was tottering. In every way that they could, the United

States encouraged the Latin American rebels. San Martin and Bolivar, leaders of the revolt in Argentina and Colombia respectively, considered themselves heirs of Washington and Jefferson. Like them they were members of the area's Creole elites, who tended to support independence for the same reasons as did the colonial oligarchies in the 13 colonies. In many places (most notably Venezuela, Mexico, and Chile) the forces of the Spanish Crown were recruited extensively from the blacks and Indians.

This was demonstrated by the first colony to declare independence: Venezuela. When the supreme Junta of Caracas threw off their allegiance to Spain on June 25, 1811, the Royalists at Valencia abolished slavery, and soon incorporated innumerable blacks into their forces. Within a year the revolt had ended. But peace was short lived.

The same year Paraguay revolted under the psychotic Jose Francia; in 1816 Argentina's elite led by San Martin pushed out the Spanish. Except for the frontier regions of Valdivia and Chiloe (loyal to Spain just as the backwoods Regulators had been to Britain in our revolution) in the south, Chile had fallen to the rebels in 1818. Bolivar succeeded in quashing Royalist resistance in Colombia, Ecuador, and Venezuela by 1819. Mexico and Peru (including Bolivia) remained loyal to Spain, even as they were the first colonized. Attached to the former was Florida:

> The Spanish position in Florida was totally untenable after the War of 1812. Deserted by the British and incapable of defending—much less administering—the Florida province, the Spanish played a waiting game. They had long since identified the man intent on their expulsion. Andrew Jackson was only the latest in a long series of conspirators who lusted after Spanish possessions. And they were quite convinced—correctly so—that he was prepared to sweep across the Gulf from Florida to Texas and

then to Mexico. Other Americans had had such dreams of empire, but Jackson, with his demonstrated military skills, was the man who could realize them.

So the Spanish waited, watched, and wrote hundreds of reports that were copied and recopied but generated nothing in the way of action to protect a crumbling empire. The first move belonged to the Americans. What pretext would trigger that move and incite Jackson and his troops into crashing into Florida the Spanish pondered and wrung their hands over. (Robert W. Remini, *Andrew Jackson and the Course of American Empire*, p.344).

The Spanish had given refuge both to runaway slaves and broken remnants of Indian tribes (the latter eventually coalescing into the Seminoles) from the United States. These would in turn revisit their former enemies to the north, raiding and pillaging, which actions the Spanish were powerless to restrain. This came to a head with the First Seminole War. On January 22, 1818, Jackson invaded Florida.

In the course of pursuing the Seminoles, Jackson seized the Spanish fort at St. Mark's on April 6. Using it as a base, he defeated the Seminoles, and then executed two British traders he accused of supplying the Indians. On May 24, he pushed on and took Pensacola, seat of government in West Florida. He then established an American military government for the region. The War in South America going poorly, the Spanish bowed to what appeared inevitable, and sold Florida on February 22, 1819. The treaty also established the border between Louisiana and New Spain. The Stars and Stripes rose over St. Augustine.

Meanwhile, as earlier noted, Bolivar succeeded in conquering Colombia, Ecuador, and Venezuela. While Mexico, Peru and Bolivia remained firm, both Bolivar and San Martin showed every intent of conquering them. King Ferdinand

VII ordered a large army to be sent to the New World in 1820 to defeat the rebels (up to this time, the King had had to rely primarily on local Royalists). But during the Napoleonic Wars, Masonic lodges had been especially formed to propagate liberal ideas among army officers. When the army was assembled to send to America, its officers mutinied, and declared in favor of a liberal constitution, which among other things was anti-clerical. Ferdinand was forced to accept it.

The generality of Mexicans refused the constitution, and the commander of the Spanish army in Mexico, General *Agustin de Iturbide* united with General Vicente Guerrero, commander of the insurgents (what remained of revolutionary forces launched by Fr. Hidalgo in 1810), in declaring the independence of Mexico. Thus, unlike the rest of Latin America, where independence came as the result of direct assaults on altar and throne by men like Bolivar, it was brought about in Mexico to defend them.

Iturbide and Guerrero produced on Feb. 24, 1821 the Plan of Iguala (from the town where it was proclaimed). This plan had three guarantees: 1) Mexico was to be an independent monarchy–under a Spanish or some other European prince; 2) Native and foreign born Spanish were to be equal; and 3) Catholicism was to be the religion of the state and no others were to be tolerated. The following August 24, the Viceroy, Don Juan O'Donoju surrendered, and Mexico became an independent empire. No European prince would accept the throne, however, and so Iturbide became Emperor Agustin I on May 19, 1822.

But influences from the north opposed the idea of a Catholic Mexican Empire; these inspired certain elements to back *Antonio Lopez de Santa Ana* against Agustin, who was deposed on March 19, 1823, and went into exile. He returned a year later, attempted unsuccessfully to regain the throne, and was executed. The next year saw the appointment of Joel Poinsett as first American Consul in Mexico.

In this country, Poinsett is remembered as the importer of Poinsettia, which is so much a part of our Christmas celebrations. But in Mexico he is recalled as the originator of "Poinsettismo," as the interference of the United States in the internal affairs of Mexico is often called there. He introduced the Masonic lodges into Mexico, and helped organize and strengthen the anti-clerical Liberal Party. From that day to this, the Mexican Liberals have always looked to the United States for assistance in battling the pro-Catholic Conservatives.

Peru and Bolivia remained in Spanish hands. Their peoples retained their ancient loyalty to the Spanish Crown.

> And loyal they were. [Latin] Americans were the majority of Spain's Peruvian army throughout all phases of the wars. At least half of the troops sent to reconquer Chile under General Manuel Osorio in 1818 were Peruvian-born. Peruvians, including free blacks in the military, had subdued revolts in the early years of the war. Peru had to be conquered militarily before it would become independent. Small towns and rural areas in northern Peru revolted against San Martin's liberating conquest. This broadly based royalist resistance included all social classes. More than one-quarter of the members of the Peruvian Congress of 1823 had to be drawn from Colombia, Argentina, and Chile. Of the fourteen Peruvian congressmen who remained during the brief Spanish reoccupation of Lima in 1823, eight switched to become Royalists. The Peruvian Congress had elected Jose de la Riva Aguero president in February, 1823. Nine months later Riva Aguero proposed to the Viceroy that Peru become a monarchy under a Spanish Prince selected by the Spanish King; in the meantime, the Viceroy would govern Peru. Bolivar arrested Peru's first traitor President. Jose Bernardo Tagle, Marquis of Torre Tagle, who had

been a deputy to the Cortes from Lima and later Inten-
dant of Trujillo, replaced Riva Aguero as President of
Peru. Early in 1824 Peru's second head of government
committed treason by defecting to the Spanish side during the second Spanish reconquest of Lima.

The masses also remained loyal to Spain. Even as Pe-
ruvian independence approached, most of the fighting
for Peru's independence was done by non-Peruvians (*Insurrection or Loyalty*, p.262).

With the majority in favor of it in Peru and Bolivia,
retention by Royalists of strategic centers (Chiloe Island and
Valdivia in Chile, Puerto Cabello in Venezuela, the fortress
of San Juan de Ulloa off Vera Cruz, Mexico) and the possible adherence of Mexican Conservatives and large groups
elsewhere in Latin America, in 1822 and 1823 restoration of
Spanish rule was not impossible. Two things were required,
however; the Liberal government in Madrid must be overturned, and Spain's partners in the Holy Alliance must give
support. Then and only then could the majority of Peruvi-
ans and Mexicans (to say nothing of the other countries)
exercise self-determination and remain under a Catholic
monarchy.

On October 22, 1822, the representatives of Great Britain, France, Austria, Prussia and Russia gathered at the Congress of Verona to consider, among other things, the revolutions in Spain and her colonies. A counter-revolutionary
movement had already emerged in northern Spain, but it
would certainly require foreign assistance to succeed. The
same was true of the Spanish colonies, whose Royalists also
needed aid. While the four continental powers were agreed
on intervention, the British government did not. The Spanish Liberals, advocating limits on the Church and Crown,
had looked to Britain for inspiration. Further, the revolutions in the colonies had opened their ports to British ship-

ping; hundreds of British mercenaries served with the rebel armies. From this time on, Great Britain ceased to be a member of the Holy Alliance.

The remaining powers authorized the French to invade Spain and restore Ferdinand VII to full power. In 1823 Louis XVIII sent the "hundred thousand sons of St. Louis" under his nephew the Duke of Angouleme, and Marshal Bourmont. The weak grasp of the Liberals became apparent when their armies melted away at the approach of the French and Spanish Royalists. Madrid entered and Ferdinand once again in full control, the stage was set for the relief of the beleaguered colonial Royalists and reconquest of those American colonies where the revolt had succeeded.

## The Monroe Doctrine

For the reasons outlined, Britain was opposed to the Holy Alliance restoring Spain's position in the New World. Knowing that the United States were of the same opinion as themselves, the British proposed a joint declaration against the planned intervention. President Monroe wrote to Jefferson asking his advice; the reply contains the following revealing lines:

> With Great Britain withdrawn from their [the Holy Alliance's] scale and shifted into that of our two continents, all Europe combined would not undertake such a war, for how would they propose to get at either enemy without superior fleets? Nor is the occasion to be slighted which this proposition offers of declaring our protest against the atrocious violations of the rights of nations by the interference of anyone in the internal affairs of another, so flagitiously begun by Bonaparte, and now continued by the equally lawless Alliance calling itself Holy.
>
> But we have, first, to ask ourselves a question. Do we

wish to acquire to our confederacy any one or more of the Spanish provinces? I candidly confess that I have ever looked on Cuba as the most interesting addition which could ever be made to our system of states. The control which, with Florida point, this island would give us over the Gulf of Mexico and the countries and isthmus bordering on it, as well as all those whose waters flow into it, would fill up the measure of our political well-being (H.A. Washington, ed., *The Writings of Thomas Jefferson*, vol. VII, p.317).

Thus we see married in foreign policy two themes which have been with us ever since: high sounding idealism masking naked greed.

Rather than ally directly with Britain in the matter, however, President Monroe instead made a unilateral declaration: while currently existing European colonies would not be molested by the US, under no circumstances would new ones be permitted; nor would reconquest of the new Latin nations. While at the time only possible because the British were resolved on the same course, this "Monroe Doctrine" basically declared to the world that the Americas were henceforth open only to United States exploitation. This would have a tremendous influence on the subsequent internal history of Latin America. As in Mexico so in the rest of the region—the Liberals looked to the US for support, while the Conservatives gazed towards a Europe rendered powerless to help them (unless the Europeans minded a war with the ever stronger United States).

The result in the immediate was that in 1824 Peru was finally forced into independence. The following year Bolivia was subjected to "liberation" with great loss of life. At last, in 1826, Chiloe, Puerto Cabello, San Juan de Ulloa, and Callao, Peru all surrendered. Spain's empire in the New World was reduced to the Philippines, the Marianas, Puerto Rico, and

*Cuba siempre leal*–"ever loyal Cuba."

Under cover of the Monroe doctrine, American interests worked ever for the triumph of anti-clericals over the Catholic interest. As a result, many Latin American Conservatives would share the following sentiments of leading Catholic Argentine philosopher Antonio Caponnetto:

> Regarding Pan Americanism and the *Monroe Doctrine* which sustains it, much has been said and written. It is, in fact, a hypocritically manipulated topic of the Left, since they *neither mention the historical support of the United States for Communism, nor do they ever mention International Monetary Imperialism* of which the United States is a seat as well as a branch but not its totality. Nonetheless, the Pan-Americanist doctrine has produced and produces fruits of perdition. In *the military order*, its big stick policy has meant the loss of territory for American nations, when there was no invasion, occupation, or support for other similar deeds. Still fresh in our memory–and difficult to erase–is the Yankee military display favoring England in the war for the Falkland Islands in 1982. In *the economic order*, systematic exploitation and the strategy of forced indebtedness has provoked, artificially in some cases, situations of dependence that imply a real obstacle to sovereignty....And, in *the legal order*, we have the creation of the OAS and other related organizations and entities that in practice only respond to the combined interests of the super-powers...

> For these and other reasons, Pan-Americanism does not constitute any serious guarantee of American unity. Above all else, there is a deeper question and it is *the explicit Protestant and Saxon philosophy that plans the extinction of the Catholic and Hispanic world vision.* This is a task for which over a long time they have been mobilizing a force worse than the military, than usury or any legal fallacies: *the penetration by sects which confuse, cor-*

*rode and consume the remaining vestiges of Christian civi-*
*lization. (The Black Legends and Hispanic Catholic Cul-*
*ture, pp.124-125).*

Although this passage may seem harsh, it were well to
compare the first portion with the quotation from Jefferson
to Monroe, and the last with this one by President John
Quincy Adams in 1826:

> There is another subject upon which, without enter-
> ing into any treaty, the moral influence of the United
> States may perhaps be exerted with beneficial conse-
> quences at such a meeting [a proposed conference of
> American nations in Panama]: the advancement of reli-
> gious liberty. Some of the southern nations are even yet
> so far under the dominion of prejudice that they have
> incorporated with their political constitutions an exclu-
> sive church, without toleration of any other than the
> dominant sect. The abandonment of this last badge of
> religious bigotry and oppression may be pressed more
> effectually by the united exertions of those who concur
> in the principles of freedom of conscience upon those
> who are yet to be convinced of their justice and wisdom,
> than by the solitary efforts of a minister to any one of the
> separate governments (James D. Richardson, *A Compi-*
> *lation of the Messages and Papers of the Presidents*, vol. II,
> p.319).

As Mary Hargreaves observes:

> Patriotism and religion marched in tandem during
> the mid 1820's, correlating the cause of developing free-
> dom in Latin America with the opening of Catholic lands
> to Protestantism and translating republican leadership
> as a mighty force to hasten world-wide spiritual regen-
> eration in accordance with God's will (*The Presidency of*
> *John Quincy Adams*, p.114).

From that day to this, it has been the same story; politically, socially, culturally, American influence in Latin America has been at the disposal of whomever has wished to destroy the heritage of Spain and Portugal (whose daughter Brazil became an independent Empire under a Portuguese Prince in 1822). It has been a long hard struggle, with American-backed forces generally triumphing in the end. But the endurance of the Catholic Iberian tradition may be seen by the fact that the battle is not over yet.

One thing has changed: the nature of the non-political forces the US backs. In the beginning, our government subsidized Protestant Bible Societies in Latin America, in hopes that Catholics would change their religion; today, although private funding from this country still assists the growth of Protestant sects in Latin America, government aid has shifted. Now USAID funds contraception and abortion. Rather than trying to get Latin Catholics to give up their Faith outright, our government will settle for their simply ceasing to practice it—doubtless in hopes that any children they may have will lose it entirely.

The change in the nature of American meddling reflects the decline of even the remnants of Christianity among US Protestants in general and the descendants of the Puritans in particular. We will see how this came about in the next section.

# UNITARIANISM, TRANSCENDENTAL-ISM, AND THE AMERICAN NOVEL

Deism or Unitarianism was the belief of Jefferson, Adams, Franklin, and others of the Founding Fathers. In 1785, King's Chapel in Boston was the scene of an intriguing election: the existence of the Holy Trinity was voted upon by the congregation. The former having lost, this one-time church of the Royal Governors became the first Unitarian church in the country. To this day, it describes itself as "Anglican in liturgy, Unitarian in theology, and Congregational in polity."

Armed with the prestige lent it by the worthy Founding Fathers, Unitarianism spread throughout New England's Congregational churches. By 1815, it had become a strong enough movement within the denomination to warrant an attack by prominent minister Jebidiah Morse. It was at the time defended by *William Ellery Channing*, minister at Boston's Federal Street Congregational Church. Four years later he assumed the leadership of the movement by his statement of principles at the ordination of one Jared Sparks in Baltimore.

As a result, elections like King's Chapel's were held in all New England's Congregational churches. Where (the majority of cases) the Trinity lost, the trinitarians would give up the old church to their opponents and move across the town common to build a new site. Where the Trinity won, the opposite occurred. But this is the reason that all over the region today one will see the First Parish or Church (marked either Congregational or Unitarian) frowning at the other on the common's opposite side. It is an almost inevitable pattern. By 1825 there were enough Unitarian churches to warrant the formation of the American Unitarian Association as a separate denomination. The appointment of a Unitarian theologian as professor of divinity at Harvard College in 1805 had already sealed that institution's connection with the new movement. Unitarianism itself became a sort of orthodoxy in New England, and was represented throughout the country—even Charleston, South Carolina boasted a Unitarian church.

Having rejected the Trinity, Original Sin, the inerrancy of Scripture and the Divinity of Christ (as well as the redemptive nature of His death on the Cross—an idea carrying with it "strong marks of absurdity" in the words of Channing) Unitarians nevertheless maintained that they were Christians. Their Christianity consisted of attempting to follow what they considered to be the moral teachings of Christ; thus they tended to continue to follow more or less the Puritan code without any real doctrinal foundation for doing so. Moreover, they continued the familiar pattern of Protestant worship inherited from the Congregationalists (or Anglicans in the case of King's Chapel) suitably altered. With those forms they continued to celebrate Baptism and the Lord's Supper as symbols of entrance into and the unity of their religious community. Unitarianism produced a belief that was rationalistic, materialistic and moralistic, but lacked fervor; in a word, it was very dry.

## The Transcendental Revolt

It is in the nature of revolutions that they must continue in stages, growing ever more radical, until at last they either burn themselves out or are put an end to. So it was with the French Revolution; so it was with the American (which continues to this day); and so it was with the religious revolution of New England. As Anglicanism gave way to Puritanism, which fell prey to Deism and then Unitarianism, so the latter must be succeeded.

The latest revolt was signaled in 1832 by a young Unitarian minister named *Ralph Waldo Emerson*. Arguing that the continued use of the Lord's Supper smacked of worshipping Christ as God, he confessed himself unable to celebrate it any longer. He declared that it was an outmoded form which, however valuable it might have been in the past, was no longer valid—at least not for Emerson himself. Since he could no longer perform the rite in conscience, he would only continue as a minister if his church would allow him to do so without it. As they refused, he gave up the trade.

Emerson was much influenced by a vast shadowy trend in literature, art and music, called **Romanticism.** Originating in Germany in the last portion of the 18th century, Romanticism opposed the ideals of the Enlightenment by declaring the primacy of the individual's emotions over the dictates of reason and the state. The a-religious moralizing of Deism came under special assault by the Romantics, who quickly spread throughout intellectual circles in Europe and the Americas. As part of their creed, the Romantics idolized nature, the (particularly medieval) past, folklore, and the far away and exotic. After the mental straight jacket of the Age of Reason and the horrors and blood of the Revolution and Napoleonic Wars, the Romantics came to have a real dislike of the here and now.

Leading Romantic philosopher A.W. Schlegel wrote:

> ...the romantic delights in indissoluble mixtures. All contrarieties: nature and art, poetry and prose, seriousness and mirth, recollection and anticipation, spirituality and sensuality, terrestrial and celestial, life and death, are by it blended together in the most intimate combination....Romantic poetry...is the expression of the secret attraction to a chaos which lies concealed in the very bosom of the ordered universe, and is perpetually striving after new and marvelous births; the life-giving spirit of primal love broods here anew on the face of the waters (*Dramatic Art and Literature*, Lecture XXII).

Such sentiments fell upon the ordered mental world of late 18th century Europe like a thunderclap. Scotland saw Sir Walter Scott evoke her storied past, while Ireland's Thomas Moore resurrected many of his country's old songs and wrote others of his own. In Germany, the Brothers Grimm gathered the stories of nursery and fireside, while E.T.A. Hoffman wove his tales of terror. France witnessed Chateaubriand compose his *Genius of Christianity*. So it went in every nation of Europe.

But out of the vast pot of Romanticism, two contradictory tendencies soon appeared. On the one hand, the nostalgia for the Middle Ages it engendered among such as Chateaubriand, Sir Walter Scott and Novalis led to many conversions to Catholicism or at least to dogmatic Christianity; in such cases political Conservatism (as summed up in the phrase "altar and throne") soon followed. The Holy Alliance was a concrete expression of such Romanticism; the English Oxford Movement which led many of its members to Catholicism and others to try to "Catholicize" Anglicanism, was another.

This was not, however, the only current stemming from Romanticism. For some Romantics, the emphasis on the individual's total autonomy and the superiority of feeling to thought led to complete disbelief in authority, whether civil or political. Such Romantics as Victor Hugo and Lord Byron came to look upon political revolution as a form of individual self-liberation and expression. Religiously, men like Schliermacher decided that faith was simply a way to evoke and express man's deepest feelings. What mattered was not intellectual belief but making contact—via the feelings and contemplation of nature—with the "spark of the Divine," whatever that might be, within all of us. This last fell heavily upon a New England made suspicious of objective dogma by its Puritan past, and of religious emotion and mysticism by its Unitarian present.

By the 1830's, "the life of the mind" pursued for its own sake was very popular among a certain set in Boston (centering around Harvard) and Concord, Massachusetts. In addition to Emerson, they included in their number George Ripley (1802-1880), Orestes Brownson (1803-1876), Bronson Alcott (1799-1888; his daughter, Louisa May, wrote a number of famous children's books, including *Little Women*), and Henry David Thoreau (1817-1862). Together they are generally referred to as *Transcendentalists*. Although Transcendentalism has been described by Perry Miller as a "sort of mid-summer madness that overtook a few intellectuals in or around Boston about the year 1840," it has had a lasting impact on our culture.

Although each held different views, they held in common belief in an "order of truths that transcends the sphere of the external senses." They rejected all external authority because "the truth of religion does not depend on tradition, nor historical facts, but has an unerring witness in the soul..." Belief in man's perfectability led them to form in 1842 a sort of commune called Brook Farm, where they hoped to demonstrate their principles concretely. They failed.

Despite the failure of Transcendentalism to function practically, its ideas nevertheless came to form with Puritan conformism and attitudes, part of the basic American character. Emerson's 1841 essay *Self-Reliance*, for instance, is filled with platitudes which have come to be part of American popular wisdom: "Society everywhere is in conspiracy against the manhood of every one of its members...," for instance, or "Whoso would be a man must be a nonconformist." From these sentiments come our national lip-service to Rugged Individualism. Similarly, generations of high school children have thrilled to Thoreau's lines in *Walden*: "I went to the woods because I wished to live deliberately, to confront only the essential facts of life, and see if I could not learn what it had to teach, and not, when I came to die, discover that I had not lived." Here we see a continuation and popularization of the notion that man is somehow set free by the wilderness. Of course, we are a very conformist folk who for the most part live in urban areas, so the attraction of such ideas is obvious. But Emerson the nonconformist was a prominent Brahmin, as the Boston WASP elite were called;

and Thoreau's cabin at Walden was a snug little retreat paid for by his aunt. Things are not always what they appear to be.

One other attitude the Transcendentalists were able to pass on to Americans was that of imbuing political issues with religious fervor. Abolitionism was the great conflict of the day; the Transcendentalists considered opposition to slavery to be a quasi-religious duty. Indeed, it led Thoreau to refuse to pay his poll-tax. He languished in jail overnight until his aunt bailed him out, but the occurrence was immortalized forever in the play, *The Night Thoreau Spent in Jail.* One thing is certain; the necessity for both sides in any American political dispute to clothe the issue in terms of a great moral crusade comes from these folk.

The Transcendentalists turned out reams of poetry and tons of essays. But one thing they generally did not do well: prose fiction.

## The Birth of American Prose

As earlier noted, Romanticism brought forth two currents; the first, the nostalgic sort, was not completely lacking in America either. By 1800, there were any number of literary elements to work with in America, in addition to the common European background. Stories of the Indians and the Revolution, English, German and Dutch folklore transformed by the New World environment, and over a century and a half of university and intellectual life all laid the necessary background for the emergence of a native American Conservative Romanticism in literature.

*Washington Irving* (1783-1859) has won unending fame as the author of *Rip Van Winkle* and *The Legend of Sleepy Hollow.* He rocketed to contemporary notoriety in 1809 with his *Dietrich Knickerbocker's History of New York*, in which he assumed the persona of an old New York antiquary of Dutch descent in order to parody the stuffy histories so prevalent at the time. An hilarious book, it was a real start for American letters, and was a first intimation that the country was truly capable of producing literary genius. In his many subsequent works like *The Sketch Book* and *Tales of the Alhambra* Irving explored the American West, Spain under the Moors, British customs, legends of his native state and many other curious things. In his work, wonder, horror, and humor were juxtaposed and mixed in true Romantic fashion according to the dictate set down by Schlegel.

Irving showed himself a true American equivalent of the Conservative wing of European Romanticism. As Van Wyck Brooks points out: "...he had antiquarian tastes and a liking for old customs and was therefore, in a sense, a natural Tory" (*The World of Washington Irving*, p.164). His artistic voice was in no small part built upon the traditions he imbibed growing up in the New York of his era:

> ...the Hudson river valley and all the country about New York teemed with legends of the Dutch. At Hell Gate, a black man, known as the Pirate's Spook, whom Stuyvesant had shot with a silver bullet, was often seen in stormy weather in a three-cornered hat, in the stern of a jolly-boat, or so it was said; and from Tappan Zee to Albany, especially in the Highlands, every crag and cove had its story. The zee was supposed to be haunted by the storm-ship of the Palisades, whose misty form blew from shore to shore whenever a gale was coming up, as well as the ghost of Rambout van Dam, the roistering Dutchman of Spuyten Duyvel, who had desecrated the Sabbath on a drunken frolic. Rambout had never appeared again, but the muffled sound of his oars was heard on evenings when, among the shadows, there was no boat to be seen, although some people thought it was one of the whale-boats, sunk by the British in the war, that was haunting its old cruising-grounds. Point-no-Point was

the resort of another storm-ship, often seen towards mid-night in the light of the moon, when the chanting of the crew was heard as if they were heaving the lead; and the Donderberg and Sugar Loaf, Storm King and Anthony's Nose bristled with legends as with trees and rocks. The captains of the river-craft, when they approached the Donderberg, lowered their peaks in deference to the keeper of the mountain, the bulbous Dutch goblin, the Heer, with the sugar-loaf hat, who was supposed to carry a speaking-trumpet. With this, when a storm was rising, he gave orders in Low Dutch for the piping up of a gust of wind or the rattling of a thunder-clap. Once he was seen astride of the bowsprit of a sloop, which he rode full butt against Anthony's Nose; and once the dominie of Esopus exorcised him, singing the hymn of St. Nicholas, whereupon the goblin threw himself up like a ball in the air and disappeared as suddenly in a whirlwind. He carried with him the nightcap of the dominie's wife, and this was found on the following Sunday morning hanging on the steeple of a church that was forty miles off. Sometimes this foul-weather urchin was surrounded by a crew of imps who, in broad breeches and short doublets, tumbled about in the rack and the mist. They buzzed like a swarm of flies about Anthony's Nose when the storm was at the height of its hurry-scurry; and once, when a sloop was overtaken by a thunder-gust, the crew saw a little white sugar-loaf hat on the masthead. This, everyone knew at once, was the hat of the Heer (Brooks, *op. cit.*, pp.48-49).

Like his European counterparts, Irving drank deeply from the legendry of his native land, transmuting it into brilliant fiction.

So too did *Nathaniel Hawthorne* (1804-1864). While Hawthorne knew the Transcendentalists (indeed, he even lived for a time at Brook Farm) he did not share their outlook. Where Irving was influenced by the often whimsical legends of Dutch New York, the shadow of Puritan New England lay heavily on Hawthorne. Descendant of a judge in the Salem witch-trials, Hawthorne produced from his native place's darker lore such classics as *The House of the Seven Gables* and *The Scarlet Letter*. It is further noteworthy that, when assuming the persona of a revolutionary war loyalist in *The Old Tory*, he wrote that it was necessary to "transform ourself, perchance, from a modern Tory into such a sturdy King-man, as once wore that pliable nick-name." He too considered himself "Conservative."

Darker still at times (although he also wrote very amusing humorous stories—not well read today) is the fiction and poetry of *Edgar Allan Poe* (1809-1849). Unlike the other two authors, he was more cosmopolitan than regional. Born in Boston, he spent five years at school in England, and lived by turns in Charleston, Richmond, New York, Philadelphia, and Baltimore. Yet, despite this, he considered himself a Southerner, and sympathized with that region in its political struggles. Whatever the setting of his stories, they owed more to his internal landscape than to their supposed location. Poe was the first American writer to be widely acknowledged in non-English-speaking countries. By the time of Poe's death, in company with such as Cooper and Paulding, these three had inaugurated a distinctive American prose literature.

All three showed (like their Conservative Romantic confreres in Europe) a certain sympathy to the Catholic Faith. Hawthorne, in *The Marble Faun*, set in Rome, praises various aspects of Catholicism, especially Confession, at great length. Irving, particularly in writing about the Spanish, whom he maintained to be, "...on many points the most high-minded and proud-spirited people in Europe," was similarly inclined. Poe, indeed, wrote a beautiful poem to Our Lady:

## HYMN OF THE ANGELUS

At morn, at noon, at twilight dim,
Maria, thou hast heard my hymn!
In joy and woe, in good and ill,
Mother of God, be with me still!
When the hours flew brightly by,
And not a cloud obscured the sky,
My soul, lest it should truant be,
Thy grace did guide to thine and thee;
Now, when the storms of fate o'ercast
Darkly my present and my past,
Let my future radiant shine
With sweet hopes of thee and thine.

Despite all of this, however, and similar effusions by such contemporary poets as Longfellow and Lowell, none of this sort of Romantic in America converted, as so many did in Europe. The reason was simply that the very idea of conversion to Catholicism, a religion so hated by the traditions from whence these folk sprang, was unthinkable to them. The only notable converts to the Faith from American Romanticism were Transcendentalists and former Brook Farmers Orestes Brownson, and Isaac Hecker, founder of the Paulist Order.

So the quest for self-fulfillment led, for Brownson and Hecker, eventually to the Faith; but Conservative nostalgia did not do so for Irving, Hawthorne (whose daughter, however, did convert, later founding an order of sisters), and Poe. Something further is revealed herein about American Conservatism.

# THE POLITICAL STRUGGLE

As literature in this period was dominated by three men, so too were politics. The first of these was *Daniel Webster* (1782-1852), a New Hampshire native whose skill at debate was immortalized in Stephen Vincent Benet's short story, *The Devil and Daniel Webster* (in which the old orator defeats Satan himself in a law-case). He began his political career in 1813 as a Federalist in the House of Representatives. In his subsequent roles as congressman (1823-1827) and senator (1827-1841) from Massachusetts, Secretary of State (1841-1843), and once more senator from the Bay State (1845-1852), his great object was the forging of the United States into a single nation greater than its constituent parts. To this end, he opposed States' Rights and the extension of slavery into new territories, and favored the right of the US government to impose high tariffs.

Henry Clay (1777-1852) we have already met as an enemy of the Faith and the Holy Alliance. Like Webster he was a zealous promoter of the Union against the States. Congressman from Kentucky at various times between 1811-1825 (occupying the Speakership of the House), Secretary of State from 1825 to 1829, and senator 1831 to 1842, and again from 1849 until he died, he was called, because of his knack for obtaining compromise, "the Great Pacificator." He favored a "National System" of roads, canals, and improvements to unite the resources of the West with the ports of the East, and generally high tariffs. On the question of slavery he favored its gradual abolition; but so adroit was he at compromise that the abolitionists accused him of supporting slavery, and the slaveholders believed him to be a radical abolitionist.

The last of the triumvirate was *John C. Calhoun* (1782-1850). A native of South Carolina, Calhoun was Congressman from that state, 1811-1817; Secretary of State under Monroe 1817-1825; Vice-President for both John Quincy Adams and Andrew Jackson from 1825 to 1832; senator from South Carolina 1833-1843; Secretary of State again 1844-45; and senator once again until his death. Unlike the other two, he retained a belief in the sovereignty of the individual states. He pioneered the doctrine of "nullification," which taught in effect that if a state government found a Federal act to be unconstitutional, it could void it by an act of the legislature. He opposed high tariffs, and sought to defend the South's economic mainstay, slavery. He was himself a kind master, and was considered to be a man of spotless integrity. Calhoun reminds one much of a Roman republican figure, austere and highly moral with no real religion.

These three in themselves summed up the regional struggles which in time would tear the Union apart. Many different political issues superimposed themselves one upon another, creating innumerable factions—a group might stand one way on the tariff issue, but differently on the slavery issue. The questions of aristocracy versus democracy, States' Rights versus Federal power, and slavery versus abolitionism, to name a few, agitated each of the States and the government in Washington. In the end, most of these questions would be solved not by agreement nor by compromise, but by bloodshed.

## Compromise and the Adams Presidency

From the end of the slave trade in 1808, New England, as we have mentioned, became ever more anti-slavery. While New York and Pennsylvania were lukewarm in their opposition (indeed, the "peculiar institution" lasted into the 1840's in New York and until 1850 in Pennsylvania), Yankee-settled states like Ohio, Indiana, and Illinois were dead set against it. By 1819 the balance was 11 slave states to 11 free states (among whom were counted New York and Pennsylvania, who were pledged to eventual abolition) thus dividing the Senate equally. As long as this was the case, neither side need fear being dominated by its opponents in the Federal government.

But this was a precarious balance. Not only were the Western territories being settled by both northerners and southerners each desirous of forming their new homes into images of their old ones (thus getting in the way of one another) but the formation of new states would decide control of the Senate. This would in turn lead either to a Federal government which would be the servant of the States—or their master.

Missouri was slated to be admitted as a slave state. This would throw the Senate into the hands of the Southerners by one vote. Since the folk of the South had shown more of the pioneering spirit than their Yankee counterparts, it was feared that they would soon fill up the West with ever more slave states. Rather than see this happen, the North was willing to keep Missouri a territory indefinitely—which, given that both sides were evenly matched in the Senate, they would be able to do. At last a compromise was worked out, to no little degree because of Henry Clay. Missouri would be admitted as a state, but so too would be the District of Maine, at the time a part of Massachusetts and virulently anti-slavery; the balance would be maintained. In addition, except for Missouri, slavery would not be permitted north of the parallel forming the line between Arkansas Territory and Missouri.

When President James Monroe stepped down in 1825, he was the last Revolutionary War veteran to hold the office (hence his nickname of "The Last Cocked Hat"). His successor, John Quincy Adams, whom we have already met, although the son of John Adams and having been a long-time Federalist stalwart, was now a Democrat—as were virtually all the other politicians. He favored a strong union, rule by the "best suited" (and so maintained a certain aristocratic tone to his administration), and opposed slavery. Favoring the same sort of National System as his Secretary of State, Henry Clay, he saw gladly the building of the famed Erie Canal which united the trade of the Hudson River with that of the Great Lakes. In this way the path of settlement in such places as Michigan and Wisconsin was made possible. He was also responsible for the adoption of an extremely high tariff—the "tariff of abominations" in 1828. This cost him the election of that year. His opponent, General Andrew Jackson, whom we last saw annoying the Spanish, succeeded him, despite a strong anti-Masonic movement which opposed Jackson. The fact that Jackson's main opponent Henry Clay was also a Freemason paralyzed them.

## The Revolution of 1829 and the Reign of Jackson

Not since Jefferson's "Revolution of 1800" had the capital seen such a change. The March 4th inauguration exemplified what many people considered Jackson's popular style as opposed to Adams'. Hordes of lower class and poor folk from all over the country descended upon the White House for a post-inauguration party. They danced on tables, smashed furniture and crockery, and in general did their best to give an impression of social revolution.

When the smoke cleared, the class system was still intact. But Jackson did intend a real change. Within his first year in the presidency, 690 office-holders were dismissed and replaced by Jackson's cronies; this is contrasted with only 74 removals by all six of his predecessors together. "To the victor belong the spoils" was his motto.

Jackson came into office with a number of interests: he

wished to move all the Indians (particularly the "Five Civilized Tribes"–Cherokee, Choctaw, Chickasaw, and his old friends the Creek and Seminole) west of the Mississippi; to end the Bank of the United States, which he considered unconstitutional (as in the beginning he was a States' Righter and friend of Calhoun, whose support had been crucial in defeating Adams); and the annexation of Texas.

The first of these goals was rather complicated. The Constitution had conferred upon the Indian tribes a sort of sovereignty comparable to that of the States or foreign nations, the nature of which, however, was not precisely defined. The Five Civilized Tribes had formed themselves into little republics; many of their citizens lived like white men, some even owning black slaves. Jackson wanted to banish them to the West by purely congressional action; they had however the knowledge to bring their case to court.

Jackson proposed Indian removal in his first message to Congress. The National Republicans (as the opponents of Jackson's Democrats now called themselves) immediately organized opposition. But the Democrats had a majority in both houses, and on May 28, 1830, the Indian Removal Act became law. It authorized Jackson to have the Five Tribes removed by the army from their ancestral lands in Georgia, Florida, Alabama, and Mississippi, and sent them to what are now Kansas and Oklahoma. Four of the tribes capitulated, but the Cherokee took the government of the State of Georgia to the Supreme Court. On March 3, 1832, that Court under Chief Justice Marshall, ruled the law unconstitutional. Jackson's reply was: "Well, John Marshall has made his decision: *now let him enforce it!*" The Indians were forced to take the "Trail of Tears" to the West; many died of hardship along the way. But they did manage in the end to rebuild their tribal governments in their places of exile.

The Bank of the United States was his next target. This

body, similar in many ways to our Federal Reserve Bank of today, held a monopoly of power over foreign and domestic exchange. Jackson felt it to be both unconstitutional and a threat to liberty. It came up for a renewal of its charter in 1832, which renewal passed the Senate on June 11 and the House on July 3. On July 10, the President vetoed it, thus ending the Bank of the United States when its charter ran out. In the message accompanying the veto, Jackson restated his belief in a limited state. But he was shortly to show that he believed rather in an unlimited one.

It was whether or not his veto should be overturned that the election of 1832 was fought against Henry Clay. Jackson won.

But no sooner was he settled down into another term, then there arose a dispute in which he showed the limits of his belief in States' Rights. Another tariff act raised the burden upon the South imposed by the Tariff of Abominations which had cost Adams the Southern vote and the Presidency. Calhoun had enunciated his doctrine of nullification in response that year. The latest tariff was the last straw. November of 1832 saw South Carolina's legislature pass an ordinance declaring the tariffs of 1828 and 1832 unconstitutional, "and are null and void, and no law, nor binding upon this state."

Jackson was outraged. On December 10, he issued the nullification proclamation, in which he abandoned States' Rights and adhered to the theory of Federal Supremacy. He further declared his readiness to enforce the tariffs militarily. Tempers flared, but neither State nor President really wanted a showdown; on February 13, 1833, a compromise tariff was worked out by Henry Clay which allowed both sides to claim the victory.

Apart from an 1835 revolt by those Seminole Indians in Florida who had refused to go into exile (and which lasted actively until 1842–some Florida Seminole not signing a peace with the government until 1962) the remainder of Jackson's reign was relatively uneventful (except for congressional squabbles in the aftermath of the fall of the Bank of the United States) within this country's boundaries. Arkansas was admitted in 1836 as a slave and Michigan in 1837 as a free state–thus maintaining the balance in the Senate.

But Jackson did encourage the activities of Americans over the Mexican border in Texas. The mercurial Santa Ana had come in and out of power in Mexico. Permitting unrestricted settlement of Texas by Anglo-Americans who fraudulently accepted baptism (at the knowing hands of one Fr. Muldoon; recipients of his ministrations were called "Muldoon-Catholics") he thus paved the way for the revolution there. (Incidentally, the Texas declaration of independence delicately describes the priesthood as one of "the eternal enemies of civil liberty, the ever ready minions of power, and the usual instruments of tyrants").

The Mexican government, becoming fearful at the influx, took steps to keep Texas an integral part of the country. The Anglo-Americans revolted, declaring their independence in the anti-Catholic document just cited. It should be mentioned for the record that they were after all foreign settlers who had been required both to convert to Catholicism and to swear allegiance to their new country before being allowed to settle in Texas. Most did so fraudulently. Did a group of Mexicans settle one of our states today, falsely convert to Baptistry or Methodism and swear a perjured oath to our constitution, and then repay our hospitality by taking the state over, we would feel betrayed. So too did the Mexicans in 1835 and 1836. Death is generally the penalty for treason, and this was the reason for the so-called massacres at Goliad and the Alamo. When Sam Houston captured Santa Ana at the Battle of San Jacinto, he intended to put the

Mexican ruler to death in reprisal. Santa Ana was to escape execution by flashing the Masonic distress signal at brother-in-the-craft Houston.

The result, however, was to bring about Mexican recognition of the independence of Texas. But Mexico considered Texas's boundaries to be the Nueces river on the South and a closely restricted line on the West; the Texans claimed everything up to the Rio Grande, including half of New Mexico. The huge disputed tract in between would be the cause of much difficulty later.

## Van Buren, Harrison, and Tyler

Jackson was replaced as standard bearer of his party in 1837 by his second Vice-President, Martin Van Buren. After the sound and fury of Jackson's reign, Van Buren's seemed a bit anti-climactic. The end of the Bank of the United States produced a yearlong depression in 1837. But while his tenure was relatively quiet, the Whig Party (organized from the remnants of the National Republicans) prepared to make a grab for the White House.

They nominated for the election of 1840 William Henry Harrison, called "Old Tippecanoe" from the site of his 1811 victory over Tecumseh and the Shawnee. He was lauded as a simple man, supposedly born in a log cabin, as against Van Buren's aristocratic Hudson Valley Dutch ways. As a result of having John Tyler as his running mate, the Whig election phrase was "Tippecanoe and Tyler, too!"

Van Buren was defeated, and on March 4, 1841 Harrison was inaugurated. But he gave a long speech in the rain, caught pneumonia, and after a little over a month in office, died. This was the first presidential death of a series: for Harrison, elected in 1840, died in office—as did Lincoln, elected in 1860; Garfield, in 1880; Mckinley, in 1900; Harding in 1920; Roosevelt in 1940; and Kennedy in 1960. All sorts of theories were advanced to explain this strange phenomenon, from Indian curses to astrological anomalies. Whatever the case, Ronald Reagan, elected in 1980, broke the series; it is just possible, one supposes, that it was all coincidence.

The death of Harrison brought Tyler to the Presidency. A number of interesting things occurred during his time which he had little to do with, but which would nevertheless play key roles in the country's future history.

Rhode Island had maintained its 1663 charter despite the revolution. What this meant was that all of the towns had equal representation in the legislature, and among them only property owners could vote. By 1840, the result was to completely discount the fact that Providence had grown enormously, and to keep the large population of artisans in town disenfranchised. Power remained in the hands of the Protestant farmers, while the largely Catholic urban workforce counted for nothing.

In 1840, a young Providence lawyer named *Thomas Dorr* (1805-1854) began agitating for constitutional change. Without being summoned by the legislature, a group elected by universal manhood gathered as a constitutional convention in Providence and passed what was called the People's Constitution on November 18, 1841. The legislature in turn called a similar convention at Newport in February 1842 and adopted what was called the Freeman's Constitution. The People's was submitted to the popular vote and accepted, while the Freeman's was rejected. On April 18, 1842, Dorr was elected Governor, but neither the state supreme court nor President Tyler recognized him. With some supporters, he went into rebellion, trying unsuccessfully to seize the state armory in Providence. This attempt was defeated, after which he went into exile in Connecticut, came back and was tried for high treason and imprisoned in 1844, being released the next year. But by that time the imposed Freeman's Constitution had been altered in many respects, and for the most part the rule of the agricultural oligarchy in Rhode Island was at an end.

An even more dramatic episode happened in New York. The descendants of those great patroons who had rallied to the revolution still retained their power in the state. Their extensive manors on the Hudson were kept with all the rights given by the King. A proprietor's tenants were bound with perpetual leases, leases for 99 years, or leases for from one to three lives. Apart from rent, the tenants had to render certain feudal services to the proprietor, and if he sold interest in a farm to another tenant he had to pay a tenth to a third of the cost to the proprietor.

Now Stephen van Rensselaer, proprietor of Rensselaerwyck, largest and grandest of the manors, had been so wealthy he did not care if the rents were paid or not. But when he died in 1839 his poorer heirs attempted to collect the monies owed them. Their agents were violently repulsed. Governor Seward called out the militia, but directed the legislature to look into the tenants' grievances. Arbitration was unsuccessful, the violence spread to other manors, and the deputy sheriff of Delaware County was murdered in 1845. In that year, an anti-rent governor was elected, who called a constitutional convention. The document thus produced was promulgated in 1846; it abolished feudal tenures. The legislature passed a battery of bills designed to break up the leaseholds, and the great proprietors quickly sold most of their land.

The results of these last two events were both local and national. On the one hand in both cases, the power of an aristocratic landed interest with primary power on a state level was destroyed. Whether or not that was a good thing depends upon how much one feels the mystic rites of the ballot box really contribute to the running of anything anyway; a case might be made that an oligarchy one can see and touch could be better than an invisible one which hides behind a faceless mass called "the people."

But the second national result was disastrous. The New York manor-lords had played an important mediating role between the interests of the Southern planters whom they recognized and were recognized by as social equals, and the governing circles of the North with whom they were also intimately connected. In good part the congressmen and senators whom they controlled had played a major role in the compromises which kept sectional strife down a bit. Now they were gone, and there were few who could speak to both Southern planters and Northern bankers and industrialists. The polarization of the regions went on all the quicker.

In 1845 the balance of states was disturbed by the admission of Florida as a slave state. This was further exacerbated just before Tyler was due to step down in favor of his Democrat successor, James K. Polk, when Texas was annexed. Not only was Texas a slave-holding region, but the republic's becoming a United State meant that the nation as a whole must inherit the territorial problem with Mexico. It was a dispute the new President wished to end in the US's favor. The stage was set for this nation's third war.

## CATHOLICISM EXPANDING

Meanwhile, Catholicism had expanded greatly since Carroll's death in 1815. Where the First Baltimore Provincial Council of 1829 was attended by the Archbishop of Baltimore and the bishops of Bardstown, Boston, New York, and Philadelphia, the sixth in 1846 saw His Grace of Baltimore joined by 16 suffragans. This tremendous growth was not brought about by mass conversions (although some extraordinary converts were made in that time) but by immigration, chiefly from Ireland, French Canada, and Germany. While such newcomers flocked to the great seaports and Northern industrial towns, various others began to establish colonies further inland, becoming an integral part of the pioneer history of our land. Often these would be led by one or another Catholic leader whose memory ought to be revered by us today. Let us survey the Catholic activities on the frontier in the period 1816-1845.

## The Louisiana Purchase

It were well to start with what had been the Louisiana Purchase. To be sure, the state of Louisiana itself hardly merited being called a "frontier" area. New Orleans was as civilized as any city in Europe at the time, and centered on its Cathedral of St. Louis fronting on the Place d'Armes–later renamed Jackson Square. Creoles, Cajuns, Isleños, Baratarians, Free People of Color, and more recent European Catholic immigrants had together evolved a unique matrix of cultures unlike anything else in the other States. Christmas, New Year's, Epiphany, Lent, Holy Week, Easter, Corpus Christi, and All Saints' were kept publicly with a fervor reminiscent of Catholic Europe and Latin America. Although the Northern part of the state was filling up with Anglo-Saxon Protestant settlers, the Creoles of New Orleans fought hard to maintain their cultural and political supremacy. But in the southern part of the state too there were new settlements. The town of Abbeville was founded by Fr. Antoine Desire Megret in 1845. He built the Church of Ste. Marie Madeleine, and laid out streets and farm plots around a central square, just like the towns of France. St. Martinville boasted the Church of St. Martin de Tours, built in 1765 and equipped with a baptismal font given by King Louis XVI. In Grand Coteau were both St. Charles College for Boys and the Convent and Academy of the Sacred Heart for

Girls; its closest rival was the similar institution run by the Ursulines in New Orleans. The Cajuns were still in the process of spreading along the bayous and prairies of the southern part of the state, while Creoles and others continued to build plantations.

Arkansas had been sparsely settled under the French and Spanish, with only a few settlers at Arkansas Post and Pine Bluff; by the 1840's, that was where most of the state's Catholics were still—and usually of French descent. But as early as 1830, Mass had been said for the handful of Irish in Little Rock.

Missouri too had a Catholic past. The old French settlement of St. Louis became a diocese in 1826, and an archdiocese in 1847. Like the Creoles of Vincennes, Indiana and those across the Mississippi in Cahokia, Kaskaskia, and Prairie du Rocher, Illinois, those of Missouri were and are a fun-loving bunch:

> Local raconteurs at Old Mines [Washington County] are especially fond of medieval French animal stories and tales of magic....At both Florissant and Ste. Genevieve, the Host is borne through the streets in a solemn and colorful ceremony at the observance of Corpus Christi in June. Christmas is celebrated with firecrackers in the southwestern parts of Missouri, and at Old Mines and Ste. Genevieve the celebration of *La Guignolée* marks New Year's Eve, as masked revelers make the rounds of homes and business places, singing a song centuries old (W.P.A., *Missouri,* p.132).

> Thomas Ashe, visiting the Creole settlement at Ste. Genevieve on a summer's evening in 1806, found the inhabitants gathered about their dooryards, "the women at work, the children at play, and the men performing music, singing songs, or telling stories..." Between numerous special occasions for group festivities, such as balls

and holy or feast days, the music loving Creoles gathered night after night for the pure joy of singing together. They sang of the tragedy of a mother who unknowingly murdered her son in *La Retour Funeste*; of the trials of love in *L'Amant Malheureux* and *Belle Rose*; and of a more reflective theme in *Le Juif Errant*. (W.P.A., *op. cit.*, p.158).

St. Charles, Missouri, first capital of the State, was the American headquarters of *St. Rose Phillipine Duchesne* (1769-1855). Born in Grenoble, she entered the Order of the Visitation in 1797. Due to the unpleasantness of the French Revolution, her religious life was disrupted; in 1805 she entered the newly founded Madames of the Sacred Heart. On March 20, 1818, she left with four other sisters to begin missionary work among the Indians, who called her "the Woman Who Prays Always."

The Creoles at Ste. Genevieve (who for a time had Audubon for their Governor) were typical of their race; we cannot forebear to delve a little more deeply into their integrally Catholic way of life:

> ...the best index of [Ste. Genevieve's] life and manners is its festivals. On New Year's Eve, masked revelers dressed as Indians or blacked as Negroes shuffle from house to house, accompanied by a fiddler and singing *La Guignolée*, an ancient French song with unwritten music and traditional words. At one time it was sung to solicit food and drink for the King's Ball, held on Twelfth Night; today, however, the masked singers demand only wine.
>
> At the *Gloria* of the Mass of Holy Thursday, before Easter, when the bells are silenced, the altar boys call the congregation to service by marching around the church square three times, rattling their rick-racks (wooden rattles) and calling out, *premier coup* (first bell), *deuxiéme coup* (second bell), and *dernier coup* (last bell). Later, in

May or June, depending on the date of Easter, the Feast
of Corpus Christi is celebrated. On this day, small shrines
are erected in front of the houses, and the town is decorated with flowers. At mid-morning, accompanied by his
assistants, the priest, bearing the Eucharist, and dressed
in the most resplendent robes of his office, leads a procession through the streets. Singing children precede the
parade, scattering flowers. The procession ends with a
special Mass and blessing in front of the church on the
public square (W.P.A., *op. cit.*, pp.269-270).

By 1845, the City of St. Louis had already acquired a
large German population. Its Greek-Revival cathedral of the
same name built in 1831-34, had been enriched by Pope
Gregory XVI with a special privilege: the same indulgence
obtained by visiting the seven Roman basilicas could be obtained by praying at each of St. Louis Cathedral's three al-
tars. King Louis XVIII of France, unable to confer spiritual
favors gave artistic gifts instead–three pictures, including a
very beautiful one of his ancestor, St. Louis IX.

Florissant, northwest of St. Louis, would be particularly
important in the history of the Church on the frontier. From
1814 on, the French inhabitants held a Corpus Christi procession similar to that of Ste. Genevieve's; their Church of
St. Ferdinand was originally built by the Spanish in 1788,
although a new stone building was erected in 1821. Nearby
was another convent built by St. Rose Phillipine Duchesne;
also thereat was the Jesuit Seminary of St. Stanislaus, where
was ordained *Fr. Pierre de Smet* (1801-1873) in 1827. We
shall see more of him in subsequent volumes. For now, let it
be said that he was certainly the greatest Indian missionary
to have worked in this country since Independence.

In addition to these long established Creole settlements,
however, there were newer German ones which formed a
pattern for later German Catholic colonies. One of the first

of these was Taos (Cole County), whose founding the W.P.A. Guide describes well:

> When Father Helias D'Huddeghem, born in Ghent in 1796, came here from Belgium as a Jesuit missionary in 1838, he found a colony of 200 Hanoverian and Bavarian immigrants in the region west of the Osage River. After four years of service among them, he gave up his missionary duties and settled in Taos, where in 1840 he had built a stone church, financed partly by his mother, the Countess of Lens, and by the Canon de la Croix of Ghent and the Leopoldine Association of Vienna. In 1874 Father Helias died and was buried in the local cemetery; his grave is marked by a tall marble shaft, simply inscribed in Latin.

> In 1847, largely through the efforts of Fr. Helias, 50 Belgians under the leadership of Pierre Dirckx, settled at Taos. They were trained craftsmen and contributed much to the prosperity of the community. Their descendants, who form the majority of the present inhabitants, preserve many religious customs not generally practiced in other parts of Missouri. On the afternoon of November 1, which is both All Saints Day and the eve of All Souls Day, a procession, headed by a cross-bearer and acolytes, follows the winding road from the church to the cemeteries, where the graves are blessed by the priest. On December 6, the Feast of St. Nicholas, a member of the congregation dresses as St. Nicholas, with a bishop's miter, cope, and staff, and, accompanied by a costumed retinue, goes from house to house, asking parents how their children have behaved during the year, and distributing candy, fruits, and nuts. On Christmas Day, after early Mass, pistols, guns, and firecrackers are shot off in the churchyard (pp.396-397).

Prior to settling in Taos, Fr. Helias evangelized German settlers in Osage and Maries Counties. Such towns as

Westphalia and Rich Fountain owe their origin to him; but
in this he was typical of many pioneering priests. In any
case, Scott County's New Hamburg possesses a similar story:

> [It is] a German community dominated by the bulk
> of the St. Lawrence Roman Catholic Church. The close-
> packed, square, one- and two-story white frame houses
> are owned by descendants of German immigrants who
> settled here in 1846. Because of their isolation, they re-
> mained a racial, religious and economic unit until a com-
> paratively recent date. On New Year's Eve, masked vil-
> lagers in fancy dress go from house to house, singing old
> German songs and being treated to wine and cakes. Be-
> lief in witchcraft is common. Spells are laid, the future
> told, and charms are often worn. Most serious is the hex
> or curse placed on individuals by their enemies. If one
> wishes to dream of a future mate, he need only sleep
> with nine different kinds of leaves beneath the pillow.
> Signs and omens are carefully observed before planting
> or reaping crops, or undertaking any other important
> venture (pp.455-456).

The center of Catholicism in Iowa in this period was
Dubuque. In 1835 Fr. Samuel Mazzuchelli reached the town
and built St. Raphael's for the local Irish and German settlers, on land donated by a miner named Thomas Kelly. Fr.
Mazzuchelli also served their countrymen in other towns on
the river, like Davenport and Muscatine. The year before he
came to Dubuque, a group of Irish farmers founded the
nearby village of Key West. Nineteen miles southwest, more
of the same group settled Cascade, where Gaelic was still
spoken into the 1930's. North of Dubuque, Germans settled
New Vienna and St. Petersburg in 1844, and with Irish settlers founded nearby Holy Cross; south of the city along the
Mississippi Luxembourgers built St. Donatus. In all of these
hamlets, the feast-days and customs of their people's home-

lands were transplanted.

What is now Minnesota was, until 1847, served by three churches only at St. Paul, St. Anthony (Minneapolis), and Mendota for the French settlers in those places.

## The Old Northwest

Of course, there was a great deal of open space within the 1783 boundaries which was being settled during these years. Let us now turn our attention to the Old Northwest. Ohio was the State of the region least affected by French settlement. Fr. Edward Fenwick was sent as first resident priest to Cincinnati in 1817. At the time the city ordinances forbade building a Catholic church within city limits. He was made Bishop of the place in 1821, after which Germans began to pour in and to transform Cincinnati from a Yankee settlement into a German stronghold. The year after Fenwick came to the state, a band of Dominicans set up St. Joseph's Priory near Somerset in Perry County. With them came a royal gift, a chalice donated by Ferdinand VII of Spain. Five years prior, German Catholics settled Fayetteville in the north of Brown County.

Indiana also obtained a large number of Catholics from abroad. For many years, of course, the old French town of Vincennes was the center of the Faith in that state. Of its people the WPA guide to Indiana says:

> The Creoles were a musical, fun-loving people, caring little for either formal government or tilling the soil. All they wanted was a living, which was easy to get in those days—hence they became known as a race of pleasure-loving idlers. Life in a frontier outpost could not have been one of complete ease, but these people always seemed to take the line of least resistance and in spite of inevitable hardships they remained gay and easygoing. Certainly they were driven by no compelling urge to accumulate lands or goods (p.273).

To a puritanical people, the charge of being pleasure-loving idlers levied against the Vincennes Creoles would have been most insulting; as it was, they simply worked to live instead of living to work. What is notable is that the Vincennes Creoles, for all that they were "pleasure-loving idlers," managed for their bishops Bruté (1834-1839) and de la Hailandiére (1839-1847) to complete the magnificent Romanesque cathedral of St. François-Xavier in 1841, to build the first library in Indiana in 1842, and to contribute mightily to the foundation of Notre Dame University in 1843.

Nor were Vincennes and South Bend the only towns in Indiana to receive Catholic foundations; in Allen County (the seat of which is Ft. Wayne), the 1840's saw the foundation of Besancon with its church of St. Louis by French immigrants. At the other end of the state, Jasper, seat of Dubois County was settled in 1838 by a band of Germans led by a Fr. Joseph Kundeck. In the churchyard of St. Joseph's, another huge romanesque structure named after Fr. Kundeck, is the Cross of Deliverance erected by sculptor Joseph Baumann in fulfillment of a vow made during a stormy crossing of the Atlantic in 1847. Tucked away in the south-east corner of the state is Dearborn County, whose towns of Dover and New Alsace were settled in 1837 by Irish, French, and Germans; the latter built in that year New Alsace's St. Paul's Catholic Church. In the same year still more German Catholics settled Oldenburg in neighboring Franklin County; ever since a center of the Faith in Indiana, it boasts a shrine of the Sorrowful Mother.

*Noel La Vasseur* (1799-1879) is an example of a great Catholic pioneer. A fur-trader, he established in 1832 a trading post at Bourbonnais, Illinois, south of Chicago. He arranged for large scale French-Canadian immigration to the area in the following decade, of which an early local historian wrote: "From Bourbonnais went people who established

every other French town in Kankakee and Iroquois counties. Kankakee in a large measure, St. Anne, L'Erable, St.
Mary, Papineau all acknowledge Bourbonnais as the mother."
In later years these folk would be responsible for the building of a miraculous shrine of Ste. Anne in the town of that
name, and two Catholic colleges in Bourbonnais itself. But
the French-Canadians were not the only folk to start Catholic colonies in Illinois. Fayette County saw a group of En-
glish-descended Catholics from Kentucky settle St. Elmo in
1830; nine years later German Catholics founded Teutopolis
in neighboring Effingham County. In 1828, the discovery
of coal at Belleville attracted hosts of primarily Catholic
Germans to the town, laying the foundations for it eventually to be come a diocese of its own.

Wisconsin's first towns were the usual French settlements;
in her case, Green Bay and Prairie du Chien. Father
Mazzuchelli whom we met in Iowa was to be the most prominent priest in Wisconsin from 1830 to 1860. Catholic immigrants came in; beginning in 1836, Germans and Irish
flocked to Milwaukee. From thence the former people spread
out. In 1843, the diocese of Milwaukee was separated from
that of Detroit. All of this was facilitated by the opening of
the Erie Canal.

The French were also responsible for the first church in
Michigan, Ste. Anne's, Detroit. *Fr. Gabriel Richard* (1767-
1832) served as pastor there for the last thirty years of his
life. He was responsible for the founding of the University
of Michigan, the first State university in the nation and went
to Congress as a delegate from the Michigan Territory. He
also worked to expand the Church outside of Detroit, as
when he bought the site for a Catholic Church in what is
now Marine City in 1824. Sault Ste. Marie, St. Ignace, and
Monroe (Frenchtown) were old French settlements which
served as gateways of migration. In 1836 a German priest

and five companions explored the wilderness in what is now Clinton County. They chose a site for German settlers, named it Westphalia, and with their help built St. Mary's Church, the State's first German Catholic parish. At the same time, missions were being established among the State's Indians– Ottawa, Ojibway, and Pottawattomi, most notably by the Bohemian born *Father (later Bishop) Frederick Baraga.*

## The Old Southwest

New Catholic settlement was not nearly so prominent in the Old Southwest–but it did occur. The "Holy Land" of Kentucky continued to grow internally, centered on Jefferson, Campbell, Nelson, and Kenton Counties. Rural folk of Maryland-English descent, its inhabitants continued to practice the plain piety of their ancestors. Among them were already such institutions as Nazareth College at Cox's Creek, founded in 1814 and the Convent at Loretto, center of the first native American order of nuns. Louisville, by contrast, had attracted a number of French emigres during their Revolution. They were followed by many Germans in the 1840's, a large number of whom were Catholic. The center of the Faith was the see city of Bardstown, whose St. Joseph's Cathedral, begun in 1814 and dedicated by Bishop Flaget in 1816, was unequaled on the frontier. Complementing its impressive classical architecture were interior gifts from King Louis-Phillipe of France, the King of Naples, and various other royal donors.

The first Catholic priests to visit Tennessee arrived in 1810. Eleven years passed before a bishop would visit the area. The first parish was founded in Nashville in 1830–and the town became a diocese seven years later. St. Mary's in that town was built in Greek Revival style in 1844-47.

In Alabama, Mobile had been since French colonial days a center of the Faith; and the Faith was similarly associated with aristocratic Creole society. Bishop Michel Portier, first bishop of the new diocese of Mobile, lay the cornerstone for the imposing Immaculate Conception Cathedral in 1836. He had founded Spring Hill College in 1830. In the coastal settlements south of the city, places like Bon Secour, Mon Louis Island, and Bayou La Batre, poor fishermen descended from the French and Spanish kept up their practice of Catholicism. In the rest of the state, the Faith was confined to large urban centers like Montgomery, where a few Catholics of good family might be found.

Like Alabama, Mississippi's coastal region was the focus of her Catholic life. Biloxi was a center of French and Spanish descendants. Other coastal towns like Pass Christian, Delisle, and Bay St. Louis all had their parishes. Natchez was made the site of a diocese by Pope Gregory XVI in 1837; the red brick Gothic Revival St. Mary's Cathedral was commenced in 1841, and would take a decade to complete.

The Seminole kept the Church, along with other institutions associated with the whites, from expanding too greatly into the interior of Florida, which after all had only come under nominal American control in 1819. The old Spanish towns of St. Augustine and Pensacola remained centers of Catholicism, as was the wrecker's settlement of Key West. Despite being a slave state, the Spanish and black mixed-bloods of Pensacola (called by that elastic phrase, "Creole") were very important socially, and bulwarks of the Faith. St. Augustine's Minorcans also retained their loyalty to the Church, and produced a number of clergy who worked throughout the Gulf states.

## The Thirteen Oldest States

Maine still counted in its Northern section as frontier territory. The oldest standing Catholic Church in New England was built by Irish in Damariscotta in 1808. The

Penobscot and Passamaquoddy Indians, who lived on state reservations had been Catholic since colonial times. Maine's northern border with Canada was not delimited until the Webster-Ashburton Treaty of 1842. With that, the British Crown conceded to the United States a number of Acadian French settlements who kept both their language and a very public expression of the Faith (Corpus Christi processions and the like) scandalous to the good Unitarians of southern Maine.

There were also in 1816 wild unsettled areas remaining in Pennsylvania, New York, and Virginia which Catholics would help to civilize in the ensuing years. In the last named commonwealth, much of the area which is now West Virginia was yet a wilderness when the War of 1812 ended. The first Catholic church was built at Wheeling in 1821, but by 1845 there were only four others: at Parkersburg, Harper's Ferry, Weston, and near Kingwood. But there are a few incidents from Catholic history there worth recalling. The most bizarre occurred at Middleway in Jefferson County, and is recounted by the W.P.A. Guide to the state in the following terms:

> According to local stories, strange happenings took place in Middleway in 1790. Adam Livingston, a settler, gave shelter to a traveler, who fell desperately ill during the night and begged Livingston to call a priest. He refused, saying that there was no priest in the neighborhood, and if there were, he would not have one in his house. The traveler died; no wake was held, for candles brought into the room were mysteriously blown out; and the nameless stranger was hastily buried. Shortly afterward horses were heard galloping around the house at night; flaming logs jumped from the fireplace and danced around the kitchen; the heads of Livingston's horses, cows, pigs, and chickens mysteriously fell off; his barn burned

to the ground; his money disappeared. Clothes, linens, and rugs, locked in chests and closets, were found cut to shreds or with tiny holes snipped in them. The snipping sound of shears could be heard night and day. Curious neighbors who called at the Livingston house went away with their clothes full of holes. Livingston appealed to his minister, but the clergyman was as mystified as the others. Finally, in a dream, Livingston saw a man in flowing robes who offered to help him. Convinced that he was a priest, Livingston went to Shepherdstown to consult Father Dennis Cahill, who returned with him to Middleway, and said Mass in the house. The manifestations stopped immediately. In gratitude Livingston deeded to the Roman Catholic Church 34 acres of ground, and specified that a chapel was to be was to be erected thereon. Trustees were appointed; years passed but no chapel was built. Livingston later sold all his property, except the broad field on the banks of the Opequon Creek, known as Priest's Field, and moved to Pennsylvania. After his death the field was claimed by his heirs; to hold the property, the Catholic Church erected about 1925 a small gable-roofed gray frame building, known as Priest's Field Chapel (pp.311-312).

Although the Hudson River valley had been settled from the 17th century, the rest of the State of New York was wide open in 1816. Starting in the 1820's, the rash of canal building (especially the Erie Canal) brought droves of Irish laborers into western New York. By 1840 they had dug 13 canals totaling 900 miles. With them came missionary priests. Beyond their announced work, these Irish "were working on the foundations of three episcopal sees, were choosing sites for five hundred churches, were opening the interior of the state to the empire of religion, as well as of commerce."

The Commonwealth of Pennsylvania was blessed with Fr. Demetrius Gallitzin, the princely Russian convert priest who established the German Catholic settlement of Loretto, and Bohemian-born St. John Neumann who would later be Bishop of Philadelphia. But perhaps the most notable Catholic effort of the period we are actually discussing was the foundation of St. Mary's in Elk County. For this town was laid out in 1842 on land owned by the German Catholic Brotherhood. It was specially prepared as a refuge for German Catholics who had fled Philadelphia and Baltimore as a result of the Know-Nothing riots; we shall look at these more closely in a moment.

## Frontier Lessons

The story of Catholicism on the frontier is very inspiring, if little known; we have barely scratched the surface. We should learn more about our fathers who came across the ocean and tried to reproduce the Faith of the lands they left in a strange and often hostile environment. They were precisely the reason for the enormous growth spoken of earlier.

But there is another, darker side to that growth. It came about almost entirely as a result of this tide of immigration—not because of conversion of the native Anglo-Americans. This was unfortunate, because starting in the 1790's and continuing for at least sixty more years, the frontier from North to South was agitated by what was called the Second Great Awakening or the Great Revival. Just as much of mainstream Protestantism today takes its lead from the Unitarians and Transcendentalists of this era, so too do many of the Fundamentalists look to Revivalism.

The relatively rapid settlement of the frontier had left many of the Eastern Protestant churches behind. Having outstripped their clergy, the settlers found themselves alone and spiritually bereft in a savage land. Starting in Kentucky about 1799, Revivalism was and is characterized by "Camp

Meetings." These were large gatherings at a given time and place; families would come from as far as 30 or 40 miles away. They would pitch their tents around a clearing where a preacher would give his version of religion. Lasting for three or four days, these meetings would include prayer meetings, preaching, hymn singing, baptisms and weddings. Very often folk were expected to feel converted and to come up and "testify" about it. Some times as many as 10,000 to 20,000 would turn out for these affairs, which sometimes degenerated into mass hysteria. The Shakers, Methodists, and Baptists profited by them to spread throughout the West; the Disciples of Christ owe their origin to them. However strange they might appear to us, they certainly showed a hunger for religion—a hunger Catholics did not attempt to supply them on any large scale.

While not attempting the difficult task of mass conversions, effort was made to interest some few. In 1844, the noted Brook Farmer Orestes Brownson came into the Church. In the next decade and indeed until his death he would be a stalwart—if not always consistent—fighter for the Faith. Theodore Hecker, who would one day found the Paulists and become identified with the Americanist heresy was a friend of Brownson and had been at Brook Farm, converted also in 1844. The next year, James McMaster (1820-1886) became a Catholic. He too pursued Catholic journalism. Unlike Brownson (with whom he differed in philosophy and politics) he was a States' Rights Democrat and anti-abolitionist.

The same year that Brownson and Hecker converted, Philadelphia was wracked by the Know-Nothing riots, which would give the first inhabitants of St. Mary's, PA, a reason to go there. The increasing flood of largely Catholic immigrants had lead in 1835 to the formation of the Native American Movement in New York. Over the next nine years the Nativists continued an ever increasing propaganda campaign against Catholics.

Things came to a head in May of 1844, in Philadelphia. A Nativist mob burned two Catholic churches in the city. In the days that followed, Catholic homes were torched, and Catholics shot on their doorsteps and hung from lampposts. They could have saved themselves and their property by hanging out American flags, or signs saying "Native Americans"; but the Nativists had made the Stars and Stripes a sign of apostasy. Bishop Kenrick, fearful that more violence might occur, ordered all the city's Catholic churches closed on May 12. He had relied on the civic officials for protection.

In New York, things were a bit different. When news arrived at Bishop John Hughes's office about the events in Philadelphia, he warned the Nativist mayor: "If a single Catholic Church is burned in New York, the city will become a second Moscow."

The mayor snidely replied, "Are you afraid that some of your churches will be burned?"

"No sir," answered the redoubtable prelate. "But I am afraid that some of yours will be burned. I have come to warn you for your own good!"

The warning served its purpose, and nothing happened in New York.

But the United States were still an anti-Catholic country, whose army was not permitted to have priests as chaplains. This was a problem, for in little while America's Catholics would once again be asked to shed their blood–this time against fellow-Catholics.

## THE MEXICAN WAR

As mentioned earlier, the annexation of Texas had made the United States heir to its new territory's land dispute with

Mexico. Further, newly elected President James K. Polk had also to deal with the British in the Oregon country. In 1818, the two nations had agreed to joint occupation of the Oregon country, which included the present states of Oregon, Washington, Idaho, and parts of Montana, as well as the southern portion of the Province of British Columbia. Both American fur traders and agents of the Hudson's Bay Company (H.B.C.) set up trading posts to fetch pelts from the Indians of the area.

The Company, which effectively administered all of what is now Western Canada as well as the Oregon Country, sent out as its "factor" or chief official one *Dr. John McLoughlin* (1784-1857) in 1824. McLoughlin was one of the noblest characters in the history of the Old West; his interest was not only to make profits for the Company, but the development of the land given to his care and the spiritual welfare of both the French half-breeds who worked for the H.B.C., and the Indians. He converted to Catholicism himself, and helped Fr. De Smet and other Catholic missionaries.

He immediately began the building of Ft. Vancouver (now Vancouver, Washington) as his headquarters. In 1829 he began the settling of Oregon City, welcoming all newcomers to the Oregon Country, regardless of nationality; he aided them all indiscriminately. As with the Mexicans in Texas, the price of such aid would be high.

McLoughlin had helped Protestant missionaries as well; in 1838 one of these returned with 50 more from the Eastern US, partially financed by the American government secret service fund. By 1841 there were enough American settlers to form a provisional government. British and Canadians were not pleased, but in 1843, 900 more Americans arrived from Independence, Missouri. The next year there were 1,400 new arrivals from thence, and in 1845 3,000. These began to show great hostility to McLoughlin and the H.B.C.

The Western States began to agitate for annexation, and at the Democratic National Convention of 1844 it was declared that the US had "clear and unquestionable" title to "the whole of the territory of Oregon." The Party, referring to the parallel which formed the northernmost boundary of the Oregon Country, made "Fifty-four forty or fight!" a campaign motto. Polk was elected on promise of obtaining it.

Negotiations were carried on, and at last it was decided to extend the frontier along the same line already dividing the two nations further east. But the whole of Vancouver Island was conceded to the British; at its southern tip H.B.C. transferred its headquarters in the new settlement of Victoria. McLoughlin ended his days in a mansion in Oregon City. Polk was free to turn his attention south.

## In Mexico

The continual tug of war between the Liberals or Federalists and the Conservatives or Centralists had continued, with the ever opportunistic Santa Ana serving as President for the Liberals. In November, 1844, Conservative General Mariano Parades went into open rebellion. Santa Ana left Mexico City to fight him; while the President was in the field, Mexico City went into revolt and the Congress deposed him. He surrendered in January of 1845, and after a few months in prison, was allowed into exile in June.

After a short period, Parades became President of Mexico. He favored the continued relationship between Church and State in Mexico, and the implementation of the Three Guarantees. One of these, of course, was the securing of a foreign prince as Emperor. Moreover, he was in favor of maintaining Mexico's territorial integrity. Thus, President Polk's ominous remarks concerning the United States destiny to expand to the Pacific were not received too well by him—any more then a declaration on his part that Mexico wished to expand to the Atlantic via Florida would have been by Polk. One thing we often forget in studying our history is that the expansion of our country has been at others' expense. Those others were quite as resentful as we might be under the circumstances.

American settlers had filtered into California from Oregon; there they would play the same part their confreres had played in that region and in Texas. After the annexation of the latter state, Polk ordered Zachary Taylor and his 3,900 troops from the Sabine River of Louisiana to Corpus Christi Bay in Texas. On February 3, 1846, Polk ordered them to move to the Rio Grande, thus ensuring the outbreak of war. On March 28, they arrived unopposed at their goal. Across the river lay the town of Matamoros and a Mexican garrison.

At first, the two armies sat. Nearly half of Taylor's forces were foreign born: 24% were Irish; 10% German; 6% English; 3% Scots; and 4% others. Memories of the outrages in Philadelphia were fresh, and the Catholics in the army were all too aware that chaplains of their Faith were not permitted in the American army. Over 200 deserted to the Mexicans. That their feelings about the war were not restricted to immigrants may be seen by this diary entry of Lieutenant Ethan Allen Hitchcock, one of Taylor's officers, and grandson of Ethan Allen:

> ...I have said from the first that the United States are the aggressors. We have outraged the Mexican government and people by an arrogance and presumption that deserve to be punished....We have not one particle of right to be here. Our force is altogether too small for the accomplishment of its errand. It looks as if the government sent a small force on purpose to bring on a war, so as to have a pretext for taking California and as much of this country as it chooses; for, whatever becomes of this

army, there is no doubt of a war between the United
States and Mexico....My heart is not in this business...but,
as a military man, I am bound to execute orders.

## The Course of the War

On May 8, the Mexicans crossed the Rio Grande, and
were defeated at the Battle of Palo Alto; the next day they
were drubbed again at Resaca de Palma. When news reached
Washington, the war would begin in earnest. A week later,
Taylor occupied Matamoros.

Meanwhile, events developed in California. General
Mariano Vallejo, head of Mexican forces in Northern California at Sonoma Presidio (whither he had removed the troops
from San Francisco), was a wealthy man. Such wealth had
come to him through using for his own purposes Mission
properties of which he was trustee for the Indians following
secularization in 1833. He had already befriended the local
Yankee settlers, insuring a place for himself under the new
regime should there be a Texas-style change of governments.
In the early morning hours of July 14, 1846, a group of
these settlers went to Vallejo's house and affected to arrest
him. He broke out drinks for all, and the California Republic was proclaimed; the flag they had already prepared for
the occasion was run up the flag-pole of the Presidio. Meanwhile, the American officer John C. Fremont, who had been
undercover, so to speak, with a party of US soldiers, took
command of the revolt. A small force of Mexicans coming
from Monterey to suppress them was repulsed, and by the
end of the month Fremont was master of all California north
of San Francisco Bay (in those days, this meant former missions San Francisco Solano in Sonoma and San Rafael, the
former Russian Ft. Ross, Sonoma Presido, Sutter's Fort in
what is now Sacramento, and many, many trees).

A few days later, on July 7, the US Pacific fleet under

Commodore Sloat demanded and received the surrender of the Californian capital at Monterey. Two days later, the USS Portsmouth which had arrived in San Francisco Bay took possession of Mission San Francisco de Asis and the deserted Presidio. The stars and stripes were raised over the plaza of the little village between the two, Yerba Buena. Today that plaza is called Portsmouth Square, and is the center of San Francisco's Chinatown.

Southern California remained defiant, however. Fremont and his California battalion were dispatched by sea to take San Diego, while a force of sailors was sent to San Pedro. Hard-riding Fremont rode quickly up the coast, joined forces with the naval party, and on August 12 received the surrender of the pueblo of Los Angeles. It appeared that California was completely in American hands.

When the city fell, Mexico already had a new president. After the defeats in the north, Parades went to assume personal command. On July 31 the Vera Cruz garrison revolted and appealed to Santa Ana to return; four days later pro-Santa Ana troops entered the capital. On August 6, Parades resigned. Thanks to American intervention, a genuine patriot's vision for Mexico was scotched, and a consummate if charming opportunist returned to power.

Two days after the fall of Los Angeles, an American column under General Stephen Kearny appeared outside Las Vegas, New Mexico, having marched all the way from Kansas. The next day the army entered Las Vegas and the small village of Tecolote; the oath of allegiance to the US was administered to the inhabitants. On the 16th, San Miguel's citizens received the oath, and the march toward Santa Fe continued. Two days later, the capital was occupied without resistance. New Mexico had fallen without a shot being fired.

Meanwhile, Taylor's men continued the southward march into Mexico. Their objective was the city of Monterrey. They arrived at its gates on September 19. The changes in government had been mirrored in the city by changes in command, which reduced the abilities of the defenders considerably. For four days they fought the Americans, but on the 24th, Monterrey, capital of the state of Nuevo Leon, fell to the invaders.

The fall of Monterrey resulted in one interesting development. More Irish deserted to the Mexicans. At length, these formed an Irish unit called the San Patricio Battalion, whose standard bore on one side the Mexican coat of arms with the motto "Long Live the Republic of Mexico;" on the other side was the figure of St. Patrick. No less than 1,011 deserted by March of 1847.

In late September, the Californios revolted against the American occupiers, and retook Los Angeles. The war in California was far from over. Fremont gathered about 430 men from the Monterey vicinity, and prepared to reconquer Los Angeles. But by the time he reached Ventura on January 11, it was revealed to him that Kearny, having marched overland from El Paso (which they had taken peacefully on December 27 after fighting a skirmish with Mexican troops) had retaken Los Angeles themselves; this after being defeated by Californios armed with lances at San Pasqual. Their honor served, they accepted American occupation.

In the meantime, Taylor's army had desultorily occupied the areas around Monterrey and Saltillo. Santa Ana had gathered a large army at San Luis Potosi, and intended to attack the Yankees at a town called Buena Vista. February 22-24, the battle raged. It was one which the Mexicans should have won. But Santa Ana was outgeneraled, and the Battle of Buena Vista proved as crushing a defeat to the Mexicans, as Saratoga had been to the British during the revolution. Meanwhile, more American troops in El Paso marched south and took Chihuahua on March 2.

This was the same day that General Winfield Scott landed with another army near Vera Cruz. After a siege, the city fell on the 29th. Then the Americans turned inland on the road to Mexico City. On April 18, Scott's troops won the battle of Cerro Gordo; two days later they triumphed again at Churubusco. With the latter, the Americans were at the gates of the city, and expected surrender. Denied this, they began an assault on the castle of Chapultepec, key to Mexico City, on September 13. By the 14th, it was in American hands.

There they annihilated among other formations the Cadets at the Military School of Chapultepec and the San Patricio Battalion. Those of the latter who were not killed in battle were hanged after capture by the victorious Americans. The battles around Mexico City are immortalized in the US Marine Corps hymn with the words "From the Halls of Montezuma..."

On the 15th, Winfield Scott's army entered Mexico City, and Santa Ana fled. For all practical purposes, the war was over. What was left of the Mexican government convened at Queretaro to await the orders of the victor. Santa Ana left the scene–to return a few years later.

On February 2, 1848, the treaty of Guadelupe Hidalgo was signed, giving California, Texas and New Mexico to the United States. The boundary was much like the one today, save that what are now Arizona south of the Gila River, and a strip including present day Las Cruces, New Mexico, remained in Mexican hands. For this, the US would give Mexico 15 million dollars. The validity of the treaty, however, required three conditions: respect for the property of the local inhabitants; maintenance of their Spanish language, culture, and customs; and freedom for Catholicism. These would be disregarded.

It would be impossible to overemphasize the impact this

conquest made on the conquerors. As Bishop David Arias points out:

> The taking of this vast region by the United States is not like coming into an uncivilized land, but into a territory that is explored and unified. It is a territory with a language and culture deeply rooted in its people and cities. Also, this is a territory with mining, agriculture, cattle raising, and economy in progress. It is a territory with its Indian population, to a large extent, settled, civilized, and Christianized from a slow but steady labor of Spain for over three hundred years. It is also a great legacy of Spain, which is now an integral part of its geographical, anthropological, and cultural identity. To realize that, one only has to formulate this question: "Would the United States be the same without Texas, New Mexico, Arizona, Colorado, and California?" (*Spanish Roots of America*, pp.256-257).

Certainly, before 1848, the mother country of the United States was Great Britain, with France providing a secondary role in Louisiana and the Old Northwest. But Spain would join the ranks of America's mother countries as a result of this war. We would be joined to Latin America from then on.

But if the war was unjust, the Mexicans had partial revenge; the newly acquired territories would worsen the sectional conflict between North and South to the point of bloodshed. James K. Polk, who had single-handedly brought the war about did not profit at all. His conduct of it created many enemies and brought about, his defeat in the next election by–Zachary Taylor, the man whose career he in a sense created, by giving him the opportunity to become "the Hero of Buena Vista."

For the Church, the problem of integrating these Catholic newcomers in the new lands was daunting. We shall see how

Church and State dealt with their new acquisitions, and the ever-increasing sectional strife in the next volume.

---

See Appendix II on p.195 for the *Treaty of the Holy Alliance.*
See Appendix III on p.199, *The French of Old Vincennes.*

# BIBLIOGRAPHY

## Part II

Adams, Henry, *History of the United States During the Administrations of James Madison*
New York: Viking Press, 1986.

Brooks, Van Wyck, *The World of Washington Irving*, New York: E.P. Dutton and Co.,
1944.

Chidsey, Donald B., *The Loyalists*, New York: Crown Publishers, 1973.

Cousins, Norman, *The Republic of Reason: The Personal Philosophies of the Founding
Fathers*, San Francisco: Harper & Row, 1988.

DeConde, Alexander, *This Affair of Louisiana*, New York: Charles Scribner's Sons,
1976.

Hackett Fischer, David, *The Revolution of American Conservatism*, New York: Harper
and Row, 1965.

Mahon, John K., *The War of 1812*, Gainesville: University of Florida Press, 1972.

Middleton, Lamar, *Revolt USA*, Freeport: Books For Libraries Press, 1968.

Smith, Joseph Burkholder, *James Madison's Phony War*, New York: Arbor House,
1983.

## Part III

Bauer, K. Jack, *The Mexican War 1846-1848*, New York: Macmillan, 1974.

Billington, Ray Allen, *The Far Western Frontier, 1830-1860*, New York: Harper and
Brothers, 1956.

Brooks, Van Wyck, *The World of Washington Irving*, New York: E.P. Dutton and Co.,
1944

Eisenhower, John S.D., *So Far From God: The U.S. War With Mexico 1846-1848*,
New York: Random House, 1989.

Hargreaves, Mary W.M., *The Presidency of John Quincy Adams*, Lawrence: University
Press of Kansas, 1985.

Merk, Frederick, *The Monroe Doctrine and American Expansionism, 1843-1849*,
New York: Alfred A. Knopf, 1967.

Niven, John, *Martin Van Buren: The Romantic Age of American Politics*, New York
and Oxford: Oxford University Press, 1983.

Remini, Robert V., *Andrew Jackson and the Course of American Freedom, 1822-1832*,
New York: Harper and Row, 1982.

*Andrew Jackson and the Course of American Democracy, 1833-1845*, New York: Harper
and Row, 1984

Shaw, Richard, *Dagger John: The Unquiet Life and Times of Archbishop John Hughes*,
New York: Paulist Press, 1977.

Smith, George Winston and Judah, Charles, *Chronicles of the Gringos*, Albuquerque:
University of New Mexico Press, 1968.

# APPENDIX I

# Loyalist Sites

## MASSACHUSETTS

*Boston:* Thomas Hutchinson, last civilian Royal Governor; Congregational Minister Mather Byles and his remarkable Loyalist daughters; the Loring-Greenough House, residence of noted Loyalist Commodore Joseph Loring, distinguished in Conquest of Canada.

*Brookline:* sites of residences of Loyalist Henry Moulton, Mandamus Councillor for the King, and a Mr. Jackson, who sold his home and left rather than quarter rebel troops.

*Cambridge:* on Brattle Street, "Tory Row," fine houses built by prominent Loyalists before the Revolution, from whence they were driven out by a mob in 1774: most famous of these–The Longfellow House, later residence of Henry Wadsworth Longfellow, but built in 1759 by Loyalist Major John Vassall; the Nicholls-Lee House, residence of Joseph Lee, Loyalist so generally beloved in neighborhood that he was allowed to return to his unconfiscated house after the war. *Salem*, the Ropes Mansion, home of Judge Ropes, prominent Loyalist whose ghost is said still to haunt the place; the Hawthorne Birthplace, where Nathaniel Hawthorne, author of several Loyalist-sympathetic pieces, was born.

*Woburn:* birthplace and statue of Count Rumford, famed Loyalist scientist. Fall River, the Old Church House, residence of Loyalist who signaled British via flags and lights.

*Wenham:* the Henry Hobbs House, built in 1747, residence of Loyalist Nathaniel Brown, who escaped attempts to tar-and-feather him by the Marblehead Company.

*Danvers:* the Page House, where the Loyalist wife, when told by her rebel husband she could not serve British taxed tea under his roof, held a tea party on the roof.

*Ashland:* the residence of Lady Agnes Frankland, widow of a Crown Official who retired to a manor-house built in the town–Lady Agnes, living alone, was forced to flee for her Loyalism in 1775.

*Littleton Center:* the Old Tory House, home of Reverend Daniel Rogers, Loyalist whose neighbors attempted to force him to change sympathies by shooting through his door.

*Royalston:* the lands of Isaac Royal, after whose expulsion for Loyalty, cultivation proved impossible on, allegedly for supernatural reasons.

*Chester:* originally Murrayfield, named after John Murray, treasurer of the proprietors, who was forced to leave and forbidden to return in 1778, by virtue of his Loyalty.

*Middlefield:* whence a number of Loyalists were expelled.

*Vineyard Haven:* the Haunted House, occupied during the Revolution by a Loyalist called Daggett, who was often visited secretly by British officers.

*Chatham:* which town voted against adoption of the Declaration of Independence.

*New Bedford:* the "Tory Houses," known by the black and white chimneys, so painted as to warn British raiders to spare them.

*Worcester:* the Timothy Paine Home–Paine, a Mandamus Councilor, refused to renounce his allegiance and toasted the King in front of John Adams.

*Barnstable:* the site of the Liberty Pole, which after its mysterious cutting down, was the cause of the tarring and feathering of the outspoken Loyalist, the Widow Nabby Freeman.

*Hancock:* home of Loyalist Richard Jackson, whose honorable nature did not permit him to escape imprisonment despite the opportunity–which led to an unconditional pardon.

*Pittsfield:* the Old Peace Party House, home of Loyalist Lucretia Williams, who to the end of her life professed her faithfulness to the King and called the Revolution "the Rebellion"; the Pittsfield Country Club, built as residence by Henry Van Schaack, driven from postmaster's position in Albany for New York for his loyalty at the Revolution.

*Lenox:* Tory Cave, refuge of Gideon Smith, one of many Loyalists in town during the war.

*Great Barrington:* home of many Loyalists, most notably magistrate David Ingersoll, who lost everything for the Crown, and was banished to England.

*Dalton:* home of the Williams Family, noted Loyalists.

# MAINE

*Wicasset:* formerly named Pownalborough after Loyalist, Dr. Pownal.

*Emery Corner* (Buxton Town): the Tory Hill Meeting House, successor to church pastored by Reverend Paul Coffin, who with many of his parishioners was a Loyalist.

# NEW HAMPSHIRE

*Portsmouth:* Haven Park, site of home of Edward Parry, Loyalist merchant whose home was attacked for unloading East India Co. tea; Pitt Tavern, until attacked in 1777 called the Earl of Halifax tavern and a gathering place for Loyalists; the Spence House, home of Robert Traill, comptroller of the port until the outbreak of war and forced to leave the province at the opening of the war. *Concord,* several Loyalists imprisoned during Revolution; the Rolfe and Rumford Home, residence of Count Rumford before his expulsion.

*Claremont:* Tory Hole, used until 1780 as refuge by Loyalists.

# VERMONT

*Arlington:* a stronghold of Anglicanism before the Revolution (its settlers had fled Puritanism in Connecticut and had the only Maypoles and Christmas celebrations in Vermont at the time), was so loyal that its neighbors called it "Tory Hollow."

# RHODE ISLAND

*East Greenwich:* location of marker where Loyalists gathered in 1774 to rout out rebels.

*Bristol:* Senator Bradford House, home of Loyalist Colonel Isaac Royall of Medford, member of the Provincial Council for 22 years–driven from his home in 1776, he nevertheless left at his 1781 death in

England 2000 acres of land in Worcester County to found first Harvard law professorship.

# CONNECTICUT

*Danbury:* the "Tory Houses," carefully marked with white and black chimneys to prevent their burning during Tryon's raid in 1777.

*New Haven:* the Tory Tavern, meeting place of local Loyalists and confiscated from owner Nicholas Callahan in 1781–now home of Yale's elite Elihu Club.

*Redding Ridge:* the Episcopal church, successor to the one headed for 50 years by noted Loyalist priest John Beach.

*Newtown:* noted Loyalist center during Revolution, another Episcopal church jointly pastored by Rev. Beach.

*Woodbury:* the Glebe House, home of the Rev. John Rutgers Marshall, nearby Loyalist rector of St. John's Episcopal Church.

*Plymouth:* Chippens Hill, Loyalist gathering place, and site of Leroy B. Pond's book,

*Tories of Chippeny Hill, Bristol:* the site of Moses Dunbar's execution (Dunbar's last will and testament is a beautiful testimony to the nobility of the Loyalist cause).

*Brooklyn:* the Malbone Episcopal Church, built in 1771 by noted Loyalist landholder Godfrey Malbone; Putnam Elms, Malbone's manor later passing into hands of his enemy, General Israel Putnam.

*Hebron:* St. Peter's Episcopal Church, formerly rectored by Rev. Samuel Peters, Loyalist cleric who, after public humiliation on village green, fled to England (where he wrote a very funny history of Connecticut in which he coined the now universal phrase, "Blue Laws").

On *Mt. Riga:* a "lost people" called the "Raggies," alleged to be descended from stranded Hessians.

*West Woodstock:* (famed stop on the King's Highway): the birthplace of Col. Joshua Chandler, Jr., Loyalist who with his son and daughter was forced to flee during the Revolution, and was drowned off the coast of Newfoundland.

*New Milford:* Tory's Hole, a cavern where local Loyalists hid from the terrorism of the "Sons of Liberty."

*Hartland:* the remains of the house of Consider Tiffany, confined to the grounds for his Loyalty for the Revolution–afterwards, he refused to leave as a continuing rebuke to his neighbors.

*Granby:* Newgate, a horrible prison where Loyalists were confined for their beliefs under incredibly inhuman conditions.

*Woodbury:* the Glebe House, where eloquent Loyalist cleric and propagandist Samuel Seabury was elected first Presiding Bishop of the Episcopal Church in the US.

# NEW YORK

*New York City:* Fraunces Tavern, called Queens' Head Tavern before British evacuation in 1783, and a Loyalist gathering place; Morris-Jumel Mansion, built by Loyalist Roger Morris and seized from him in 1783.

*Amsterdam:* Guy Park, home of Loyalist leader Colonel Guy Johnson, nephew and son-in-law of Sir William.

*The Bronx:* Vault Hill, grave of Augustus Van Cortlandt, member of the manorial family, clerk of the Common Council of New York, and sole prominent member of his family to remain loyal; Edenwald, a section formerly comprising the estate of the Seton Family, descended from Mary Seton, of Mary Queen of Scots' "four Maries," Loyalists in the Revolution, and among whom by marriage was St. Elizabeth Seton, first native-born American Catholic saint.

*Queens:* home to a large number of Loyalists who emigrated to Newfoundland in 1783.

*Staten Island:* the Conference House, where Howe and Washington held a parley in 1776, it was owned by Loyalist Colonel Thomas Billopp; the Kreuzer-Pelton House, used as headquarters during the Revolution by Loyalist militia leader Cortlandt Skinner.

*Fort Johnson:* Ft. Johnson, stronghold of Loyalist Johnson clan, founded by Sir William Johnson, Joseph Brant's brother-in-law.

*Johnstown:* their other home, Johnson Hall–from it Sir William's son, Sir John, fled with 700 tenants (some of whom later joined his two battalions of "Royal Greens") to Montreal in May of 1776.

*Fonda:* Butler House, center of Butlersbury Manor, home of Walter Butler, organizer of the Loyalist regiment, Butler's Rangers.

*Palatine Ridge:* Palatine Church, built by German settlers in 1770–one of the families responsible for it were the Nellises, whose loyalties were split in the Revolution: it was saved by a Loyalist member of the family during a raid, and to this day Nellises from Canada attend the annual reunion held here.

*Schenectady:* St. George's Episcopal Church, reputed grave of Loyalist chief Walter Butler (Butler's Rangers), secretly buried there in 1781.

*Yonkers:* Philipse Hall, center of Philipsburgh Manor, granted by William III in 1693 to Frederick Philipse: and confiscated from his Loyal great grandson in 1779.

*Sloatsburg:* nearby the Ramapo Mountains, in which, as over the border in New Jersey, are the "Jackson Whites."

*Tuxedo:* the Claudius Smith Caves, named after the leader of a band of Loyalist raiders who operated from them.

*Van Cortlandtville:* Gallows Hill, where Loyalist spy Edward Palmer was hanged in 1777 by order of General Israel Putnam.

*Sharon Center:* headquarters for Loyalists under Captain John Dockstader until their defeat by rebels in 1781.

*Cherry Valley:* site of a victory against the rebels by Loyalists and Indians under Walter Butler and Mohawk chief Joseph Brant.

*Cobleskill:* site of a victory against the rebels by Loyalists and Indians led by Joseph Brant.

*Ft. Plain:* Indian Castle Church, last remaining part of Chief Joseph Brant, head of the Loyal Mohawks.

*Whitehall:* site of Skenesborough, manor of Loyalist Major Philip Skene, who after losing all to the rebels, guided Burgoyne through the area.

*North Tarrytown:* Castle Philipse, owned by the Loyalist lord of Philipseburgh Manor, and like it confiscated by the rebels.

*Oyster Bay:* Raynham Hall, headquarters of Loyalist Lieutenant Colonel John Simcoe and his Queen's Rangers.

*Massapequa:* Tryon Hall, home of Loyalist Judge Thomas Jones.

*Poughkeepsie:* the Glebe House, residence of Christ Episcopal Church's first rector, Reverend John Beardsley, from 1767 to 1777, when he was exiled for his Loyalism; he was rector also of Trinity Episcopal Church in Fishkill Village.

# NEW JERSEY

*New Brunswick:* center of Loyalist sentiment, with site of Cochrane's Tavern, owned by well-known Loyalist Bernardus Le Grange, whose effigy was burned and property seized.

*Elizabeth:* The Old Chateau, home of the Cavalier Jouet who lost it due to his loyalty to George III. Morristown, the Kemble House, built in 1750 by noted Loyalist Dr. Peter Kemble.

*Newton:* Moody's Rock, refuge of a band of Loyalist raiders led by James (Bonnel) Moody, whose account of their adventures was published in London in 1783.

*Verona:* a town owned originally by Loyalist Caleb Hetfield. Butler, a large number of whose people descend from Hessian troops who elected to stay after the Revolution ended.

*Ringwood:* center for the Ramapo Mountains, inhabited by the "Jackson Whites" descendants of British Camp Followers expelled from New York after that city's evacuation by the British in 1783, stranded Hessians, blacks, and Indians–some spoke Dutch as late as 1905.

*Spotswood:* ruins of pioneer iron works owned by Loyalists, confiscated and allowed to fall apart by the rebel state authorities.

*High Bridge:* site of Taylor Home, where John Penn, last Royal Governor of Pennsylvania and descendant of William was held prisoner for six months in 1776 on order of the Continental Congress.

*River Edge:* the Steuben House, owned by the Loyalist Zabriskie brothers, it was confiscated from them and given in 1783 as a reward to Baron von Steuben–he in turn sold it back to the Zabriskies.

*Nutley:* whose main street bears the name Franklin in honor of Governor William; the Old Nutley Manor, seized from Loyalist owners.

*Toms River:* site of Loyalist raid which ended in hanging of notorious anti-Loyalist Capt. Joshua Huddy by victims of his depredations–in reprisal Washington ordered hanging of a British officer, to avoid which General Sir Guy Carleton apologized and dissolved the Loyalist organization responsible.

*Shacks Corner:* Our House Tavern, stronghold of one Fenton, leader of a local band of Loyalist raiders'; Fagin's Cave, another such hideout.

*Colt's Neck:* Colt's Neck Inn, onetime property of the Notorious Captain Josua Huddy, once besieged here by 60 Loyalists led by ex-slave Col. Titus Tye; in the area south of the town were several bands of Loyalists called "Pine Robbers." Allenwood, granite marker commemorating the execution of seven Loyalists. Pine Barrens, region inhabited by so-called "Pineys," whose ancestors were forced to flee to this desolate region for their Loyalty.

*Hancock's Bridge:* the William Hancock, where Loyalist Judge Hancock was mistakenly killed by fellow Loyalists under Major John Simcoe who were attacking the rebels occupying the house.

*Greenwich:* site of Greenwich tea party, when town's Loyalists attempted to save tea bound for Philadelphia from destruction.

# PENNSYLVANIA

*Philadelphia:* the University of Pennsylvania, whose initial endowment fund after rechartering as a republican institution was made up of the proceeds from 60 confiscated Loyalist estates; the residence here of noted Tory Radical William Cobbett; the Randolph Mansion, home of Samuel Shoemaker, Loyalist mayor of Philadelphia, who left with the British in 1778; Ormiston Mansion, built in 1798 on confiscated estate of Joseph Galloway, Loyalist politician, theorist, and philosopher.

*Langhorne:* the Hicks House, where Royal official Gilbert Hicks read General Howe's Amnesty Proclamation on 30 November 1776–for which act he was forced to flee.

*Allentown:* Trout Hall, place of house arrest for James Hamilton, Loyalist cousin of Benjamin Franklin.

*Bristol:* the Delaware House Hotel, originally George II Hotel until Rebel soldiers forcibly changed the name.

*Maytown:* Donegal Presbyterian Church, whose Loyalist pastor, the Reverend Mr. McFarquar, was made to lift his hat to the Revolution at gunpoint.

*Neshaminy:* Graeme Park and the Keith House, owned by Loyalist Henry Fergusson, who served with the British and was convicted of High Treason in absentia.

*Snowshoe Mountain:* home of the "Mountaineers," a people who descend in part from ancestors driven out of the valleys for their loyalty to the King.

*Germantown:* Chew Mansion, residence of noted Loyalist Benjamin Chew.

# DELAWARE

*Lewes:* the site where 1,000 Loyalists gathered on 11 June 1775 to fight for the King–they dispersed after assurances that the rebel leaders wanted redress, not independence.

*Milford:* the home of Parson Sydenham Thorne, rector of Christ Church, who despite his loyalty was so beloved that he was left unmolested until his death in 1793.

*Middletown:* Old St. Anne's Episcopal Churchyard, with grave of Loyalist rector Rev Philip Reading.

*Leipsic:* Pleasanton Abbey, gathering place of Loyalists under local leader Henry Stevens.

*Down's Chapel:* the site of the fort of Cheney Clow, local Loyalist chief, hanged after the war.

# MARYLAND

*Annapolis:* Masonic Temple, built in 1770 as home of Lloyd Dulany, prominent Loyalist and kinsman of Loyalist writer Daniel Dulany–confiscated by State.

*Baltimore:* St. Paul's Churchyard, with grave of prominent Loyalist, Daniel Dulany.

*Frederick:* the site of the Tory Gaol, where, of seven prominent Loyalists imprisoned here in 1780, three were hanged, drawn, and quartered.

Near *Bertha:* Point Patience Manor, granted to John Aschcomb (Ascham) in 1661, and confiscated from the Aschams at the time of the Revolution as a result of their loyalty.

Near *Davidsonville:* St. Barnabas Episcopal Church and Mt. Lubentia, living and residence 1770-1774 of noted Loyalist Rev. Jonathan Boucher.

*Keysville:* Terra Rubra, birthplace of Francis Scott Key (author of the "Star-spangled Banner"), and of his Loyalist uncle, owner of half the estate who joined the British army during the Revolution.

# VIRGINIA

*Williamsburg:* Tazewell Hall, residence of John Randolph, Attorney General for the colony, and unlike his brother and son, so staunch a Loyalist that he left for England at the outbreak of hostilities.

*Norfolk:* so filled with Loyalists that after the last Royal Governor, Lord Dunmore, was forced out of the town, the rebels burned all save the Episcopal Church.

*Portsmouth:* home of Loyalist merchant Andrew Sprowle, who gave refuge to Lord Dunmore after he fled Norfolk–upon the latter's withdrawal, the rebels torched Portsmouth as they had Norfolk.

*Winchester:* Christ Episcopal Church, in churchyard, grave of Loyalist Lord Fairfax, proprietor of the Northern Neck of Virginia. King And Queen, site of Laneville, home of Loyalist Richard Corbin.

*Whitepost:* Greenway Court, home of Loyalist proprietor, Lord Fairfax.

*Gwynn's Island:* site of Lord Dunmore's last stand in Virginia.

*Great Bridge:* site of battle between Lord Dunmore's men and the rebels, which allowed the latter to seize the land approach to Nor-folk.

*Kempsville:* home of Loyalist George Logan, where Governor Dunmore rallied the locals to the King's colors.

*Amelia:* St. John's Episcopal Church, whose Loyalist rector, Reverend John Brunskill, was not allowed by his rebel parishioners to hold services, but lived on in the glebe house until his death in 1803.

*Westover Plantation:* home of the Loyalist Byrd Family, whose mate-rial aid to the British was so carefully concealed that they did not lose Westover as a result.

# WEST VIRGINIA

*Romney:* center of operations of a Loyalist company led by John Claypole.

# NORTH CAROLINA

*New Bern:* Christ Episcopal Churchyard, with grave of Reverend James Reed, Loyalist first rector.

*Edenton:* the Cupola House, formerly the scene of large celebrations of the King's birthday, and possessing, on a fireback, a likeness and the arms of George II in bas-relief.

*Wilmington:* Lilliput Plantation and Old Palace Field, properties owned by Josiah Martin, last Royal Governor, and confiscated by the rebels.

*Fayetteville:* residence for a few months in 1774 of Flora MacDonald, heroine of Bonnie Prince Charlie's 1746 flight after Culloden, and her husband, Col. Allan MacDonald, who commanded the local Jacobite Scots settlers in the King's interest at the opening of the Revolution; Cool Spring, where Flora rallied the Highlanders for King George.

*Southport:* Ft. Johnston, refuge of Governor Josiah Martin after he was forced out of New Bern, and until driven out by rebels.

*Colerain:* Mill Landing Farm, owned by the Loyalist Duckenfield Family until their expulsion.

*Halifax:* the Old Gaol, where 41 Scots Highland leaders including Col. Allan MacDonald, were imprisoned after their defeat by the rebels at Moore's Creek Bridge in March 1776.

*Raeford:* site of battle of McFall Mill or Raft Swamp on 1 September 1781—a rebel force was defeated by Loyalists under Colonels Ray,

McDougal, David Fanning, and "Sailor" Hector McNeill.

*Pittsboro:* Chatham County Court House, site of raid and daring rescue by Loyalists led by Davi Fanning while a court-martial trying other Loyalists was in session.

*Cross Hill:* site where Loyalists rendezvoused in February 1776 under General Donald MacDonald and Colonel Allan MacDonald.

*Hillsboro:* raided by Loyalists under David Fanning and Hector McNeill on 13 September 1781.

*Red Springs:* built on land granted to Colonel Hector McNeill, Loyalist chief, many of whose descendants still reside here.

*Moore's Creek Bridge National Military Park:* site of battle on 27 February 1776 between Loyalist-Jacobite Scots under General Donald MacDonald and Colonel Allan MacDonald and rebels—the defeat of the former prevented their linking up with Governor Josiah Martin's forces and putting an end to the rebellion in North Carolina.

*Wilkesboro:* the Tory Oak, from which five Loyalists were hanged by rebel Colonel Benjamin Cleveland—one of these, William Riddle, had spared Cleveland's life under similar circumstances.

*Elizabethtown:* Tory Hole, near site of August 1781 battle of Elizabethtown, where Loyalists fled after defeat.

## SOUTH CAROLINA

*Greenville:* the home of Colonel Richard Pearis, daring Loyalist militia leader.

*Traveler's Rest:* center of operations of Loyalist guerrilla leader, William Bates.

*Chesnee:* named after the Loyalist Chesney Family, one of whom, Andrew, wrote a famous journal of his experiences in the Revolution.

*Waterloo:* site of Rosemont Manor, home of the Cunninghams, a Loyalist family led by Patrick, to whom George III granted the land in 1769—they were able to return after a sojourn in the West Indies.

## GEORGIA

*Savannah:* the McIntosh House, which as Eppinger's Inn was a Loyalist meeting place.

*Augusta:* takeover of town in 1780 by Loyalist colonels Grierson and Browne, the latter of whom had been tarred-and-feathered there by a rebel mob five years previously—they successfully endured a four day siege in the Old White House after a rebel counterattack in September.

*Rincon:* the site of Mulberry Grove Plantation, owned by Lieutenant Governor John Graham, but confiscated after the Revolution and given to rebel General Nathanael Greene.

## FLORIDA

*St. Augustine:* the first Floridian newspaper, the *East Florida Gazette,* published by Loyalist Charlestonian William Charles Wells.

*Riviera:* mixed blood (English, black, Indian) Conchs–descendants of Loyalists who fled to the Bahamas.

*Key West:* white Conchs, likewise Loyalist descendants.

## WISCONSIN

*Green Bay:* French and British settlers remained loyal to Crown during both Revolution and War of 1812, many serving in both wars against Americans–US control only established in 1816; home of Charles Michel de Langlade (1729-1800), who led Indians against the rebels during the Revolution.

## MISSISSIPPI

*Natchez:* a refuge for Loyalists fleeing the Revolution, until American occupation in 1798.

*Guntown:* named for Virginia Loyalist James Gunn, who fled here, married the daughter of a Chickasaw Indian chief, and toasted the King on the latter's birthday until he died.

## LOUISIANA

*East* and *West Feliciana Parishes:* descendants of Loyalists who fled US rule after the Revolution.

## ONTARIO

*Niagara-On-The-Lake:* originally named Butlersburg after Col. John Butler, commander of New York Loyalist regiment, Butler's Rangers, and who lies buried here in Butler's Burial Ground.

*Brantford:* refuge of Loyalist Mohawks under their chief, Joseph Brant;
Her Majesty's Chapel of the Mohawks, built in 1785, and possessing the communion service given the tribe by Queen Anne when
they were in New York.

*Desoronto:* named for Mohawk chief Capt. Desoronto, who lead a
band of his loyal tribesmen to the spot after the Revolution; their
descendants remain in the nearby reserve of Tyendinaga.

*Cornwall:* originally named New Johnstown, it was settled in 1784 by
veterans of Sir John Johnston's Royal Regiment of New York; plaque
at Post Office commemorates their gallantry.

*Williamstown:* named after Sir William Johnston, father of Sir John;
here is the manor house built by the latter in 1784.

*St. Raphael's:* settled by veterans of Sir John's Royal Highland Emi-
grants in 1784.

# NEW BRUNSWICK

*Saint John:* founded by New England Loyalist refugees in 1783; Trinity Anglican Church, with wooden Royal coat-of-arms, formerly in
the Council Chamber of the Old State House in Boston; the Loyalist House, built in 1817 with many souvenirs of the Loyalists in
New Brunswick.

*St. Andrews:* settled by United Empire Loyalists in 1783, and preserv-
ing the blockhouse they built for protection.

# NOVA SCOTIA

*Shelburne:* settled in 1783 by 10,000 Loyalists; the Ross-Thompson
House, Loyalist Museum.

# APPENDIX II

# Treaty of The Holy Alliance

In the name of the Most Holy and Indivisible Trinity.

## Holy Alliance of Sovereigns of Austria, Prussia, and Russia.

Their Majesties the Emperor of Austria, the King of Prussia, and the Emperor of Russia, having, in consequence of the great events which have marked the course of the three last years in Europe, and especially of the blessings which it has pleased Divine Providence to shower down upon those States which place their confidence and their hope in it alone, acquire the intimate conviction of the necessity of settling the steps to be observed by the Powers, in their reciprocal relations, upon the sublime truths which the Holy Religion of our Savior teaches;

## Government and Political Relations.

They solemnly declare that the present Act has no other object than to publish, in the face of the whole world, their fixed resolution, both in the administration of their respective States, and in their political relations with every other Government, to take for their sole guide the precepts of that Holy Religion, namely, the precepts of Justice, Christian Charity and Peace, which, far from being applicable only to private concerns, must have an immediate influence on the councils of Princes, and guide all their steps, as being the only means of consolidating human institutions and remedying their imperfections. In consequence, their Majesties have agreed on the following articles:—

## Principles of the Christian Religion.

**Art. I.** Conformably to the words of the Holy Scriptures which command all men to consider each other as brethren, the Three contracting Monarchs will remain united by the bonds of a true and indissoluble fraternity, and considering each other as fellow countrymen, they will, on all occasions and in all places lend each other aid and assistance; and, regarding themselves towards their subjects and armies as fathers of families, they will lead them in the same spirit of fraternity with which they are animated, to protect Religion, Peace, and Justice.

## Fraternity and Affection.

**Art. II.** In consequence, the sole principle of force, whether between the said governments or between their Subjects, shall be that of doing each other reciprocal service, and of testifying by unalterable good will the mutual affection with which they ought to be animated, to consider themselves as all members of one and the same Christian nation; the three allied Princes looking on themselves as merely delegated by Providence to govern three branches of the One family, namely Austria, Prussia and Russia, thus confessing that the Christian world, of which they and their people form a part, has in reality no other Sovereign than Him to whom alone power really belongs, because in Him alone are found all the treasures of love, science and infinite wisdom, that is to say, God, our Divine Savior, the Word of the Most High, the Word of Life. Their Majesties consequently recommend to their people, with the most tender solicitude, as the sole means of enjoying that Peace which arises from a good conscience, and which alone is durable, to strengthen themselves every day more and more in the principles and exercise of the duties which the Divine Savior has taught to mankind.

## Accession of Foreign Powers.

Art. III. All the Powers who shall choose solemnly to avow the sacred principles which have dictated the present Act, and shall acknowledge how important it is for the happiness of nations, too long agitated, that these truths should henceforth exercise over the destinies of mankind all the influence which belongs to them, will be received with equal ardor and affection into this Holy Alliance.

# APPENDIX III

# The French of Old Vincennes

The most distinctive national group of Indiana was the early French Creoles who settled along the Wabash River. To the pioneer making his way along the river highways into the wilderness, the wide savannah at Post Vincennes presented a novel picture as it lay spread out before him. Each thatched white cottage was surrounded by its own garden, where the family raised enough food to last the year around. Surplus food was shipped by flatboat to New Orleans. Produce from outlying gardens was brought to the market in the *caléche*, a two-wheeled cart made entirely of wood, the first vehicle in the old Northwest Territory.

Flatboatmen returning semiannually from New Orleans were welcomed with great joy. It was then that all the new songs learned by the men during their voyage were sung. The songs were long, so each man learned a line of the verse and all learned the chorus. Instead of singing the song through, each man sang his line, and after each line, all joined in the chorus. On these occasions, people stayed up all night learning the songs. These trips to New Orleans were the settlement's only contact with the outside world.

During the holiday balls and at the singings held in the

homes, the Creoles sang all their songs. Some of the favorites were *Au Clair de la Lune*, *Mon Amour*, and *La Belle Françoise*. After the sad strains of *La Belle Françoise*, they paused in silence. *Kersie* was the last song sung at the traditional Christmas King Ball of Old Vincennes. Lovers who had quarreled then made up and walked home together.

New Year was the great Creole holiday. Festivities began with New Year's Eve. The following day masqueraders went from house to house singing and playing old songs and dramas. Early New Year's morning each Creole went to visit the oldest member of his family, and the older people were in turn hosts throughout the day. Each visitor kissed all members of the family.

Many folksongs had a special meaning and use. *L'Alouette* was sung when the French women prepared chickens for the feast. Other songs were *Rose d'Amour* and *Mon Berger*. *La Gui Année*, or the *Beggar's Song*, referred to the New Year mistletoe.

As late as 1855 the French controlled elections in Knox County. The Indian strain in these early citizens was easily discernible in the high cheek bones and straight black hair of many Creoles. The common attire of the men consisted of buckskin coat, knee breeches, and leggings. During the winter they added moccasins and a *capote,* a long hooded overcoat made of fur. Neither men nor women wore shoes in the summer. The most common garment worn by the women was the *habit*, reaching to the knees; under it was usually worn a petticoat that hung down to the ankles. Both sexes were fond of bright colors around the throat and waist, and costumes were often decorated with bright beads in the Indian fashion (*op. cit.,* pp.272, 273).